Susan L. Lingo

COLLECT-N-Play
GaMeS
for Kids

Standard®
PUBLISHING
Bringing The Word to Life

Cincinnati, Ohio

Dedication

**But thanks be to God! He gives us the victory
through our Lord Jesus Christ.**

1 Corinthians 15:57

Collect-n-Play Games for Kids
Copyright © by 2001 Susan L. Lingo

Published by Standard Publishing, Cincinnati, Ohio
www.standardpub.com

Credits
Produced by Susan L. Lingo, Bright Ideas Books™
Cover design by Diana Walters
Illustrated by Paula Becker

08 07   5 4
ISBN-13: 978-0-7847-1199-6
ISBN-10: 0-7847-1199-2
Printed in the United States of America

CONTENTS

GAME SECTIONS

Medium- to low-energy games and cooperative playtimes
for indoors in a classroom, gymnasium, or fellowship hall.

High- to medium-energy relays, races, games, and water play
for outdoor fun in the sun or shade.

A variety of games and active competitions and cooperative
activities able to be played in 5-7 minutes or less.

Low-energy games to keep kids calm and quiet and help
them refocus their attention.

NOW, GREAT GAMES ARE AS SIMPLE AS 1-2-3 WITH
Collect-n-Play Games for Kids!

Get ready to play oodles of fun games with powerful biblical messages—in just three easy steps. Collect eighteen everyday items (or sets of items); place them in a bag, box, or basket along with this copy of *Collect-n-Play Games for Kids*; and you're ready to play over sixty super games, raucous relays, lively races, and much more. But don't be fooled! These aren't just play-'em-and-forget-'em games; they are games with powerful Bible messages that get God's Word across in memorable ways that engage kids' minds, hearts, and bodies. You might call it *fun with a focus*! Your kids will delight in the wide variety of games that encourage cooperation, communication, and team building. And with the Game Kit and this book at hand, you can play these super games at a moment's notice or take them along to VBS playtimes, family picnics, and church retreats. Simply follow these three easy assembly-in-a-snap directions....

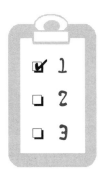

COLLECT EVERYDAY ITEMS. Check your garage, kitchen, or attic for the everyday items listed on page 7. Check off the items as they're collected. You may wish to photocopy the list and place it in a spot where church members can see what's needed and then donate the items. Be sure to place a decorated box below the list to hold the collections. (Your kids might even wish to make an announcement to the entire church asking for donations.) If enough extra items are contributed, consider making a second Game Kit and purchasing another copy of *Collect-n-Play Games for Kids* to add to the kit. Present your super service project to a children's home or Head Start program center. What a great way to get God's Word to others in a fun way!

PLACE THE GAME-KIT ITEMS IN A BAG, BOX, OR BASKET. Let kids help decorate a box with a lid to hold your collected playing items. Colorful self-adhesive paper, gift wrap, or even rolled adhesive cork work well to cover the box. (You will want something sturdy to last for years of playtime fun and learning!) Or consider using a large mesh bag—the kind that normally holds laundry—or even a bright, plastic laundry basket as a kit to hold your playing items. Don't forget to keep a copy of the Bible and *Collect-n-Play Games for Kids* in your Game Kit!

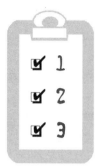

RACE, RUN, AND PLAY AWAY! Believe it or not, you're all set to play a super selection of games that will soon become your kids' new favorites. You'll want to be sure to set up one of the simple, ingenious indoor game-floor setups for the section titled "Indoor Delights." Illustrations for the one-time setup are found on page 8.

DIRECTIONS FOR MAKING THE ROLLING CUBE, BEANBAG SOCKS, AND TABLE-TENNIS BALLS

✔ Make the **rolling cube** from a square box with all its sides intact. (Be sure the box will fit in your Game Kit.) Cover or color each side of the box with one each of the following colors: pink, blue, green, red, yellow, and purple. Finally, use a permanent marker to number the sides from 1 to 6. If you wish, cover the box with clear, self-adhesive paper for added durability.

✔ Make a **beanbag sock** by pouring small, dried beans or peas into the foot portion of a sock. Fill half the foot section, then tie the sock in a knot above the dried beans. Cut away excess material.

✔ Use a permanent marker to number the **table-tennis balls** from 1 to 4.

PLAYING ITEMS FOR
Collect-n-Play Games for Kids

Collect the following items or sets of items and place them in a large bag, box, or basket to play over sixty super games with a focus on God's Word. Check off the items as they're collected.

❑ 1 Bible

❑ 1 copy of *Collect-n-Play Games for Kids*

❑ 4 colored plastic plates (lightweight type used for picnics)

❑ 1 stopwatch or kitchen timer

❑ 1 beach ball

❑ 1 package of small to medium balloons

❑ 4 10-inch fabric squares (scarves or bandannas will work)

❑ 1 package of paper plates

❑ 4 table-tennis balls (see page 6)

❑ 4 paint stir sticks

❑ 8 colored plastic tumblers

❑ 1 roll of masking tape

❑ 1 package of plastic spoons

❑ 1 package of index cards

❑ 1 package of cotton balls

❑ 1 pack of 24 crayons

❑ 1 long jump rope

❑ 2 beanbag socks (see page 6)

❑ 1 rolling cube (see page 6)

INDOOR GAME-FLOOR SETUPS

SQUARE GAME FLOOR

CIRCLE GAME FLOOR

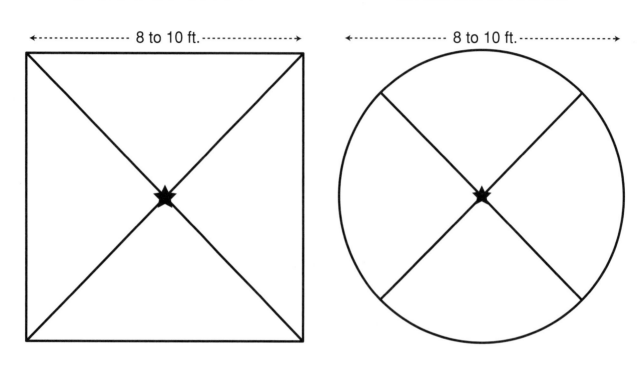

OBLONG GAME FLOOR

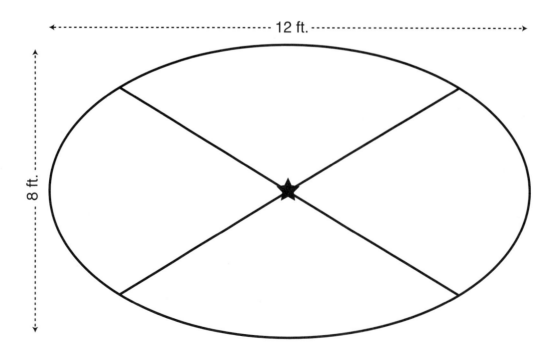

Section 1:

INDOOR DELIGHTS

- ☑ rainy-day relays
- ☑ classroom contests
- ☑ partner play
- ☑ and more!

It's raining, it's pouring—indoor games are boring!

Not any longer! Here's a collection of indoor games to delight and excite your playful crew even on the stormiest of days. Relays, races, juggling, tossing, and partner-play create lively, happy playtimes anytime. And with the cool indoor game floor (see page 8), you'll be ready to play in a snap. Choose the game-floor diagram that best fits your space and shape requirements, then use masking tape or colored electrical tape to lay the lines and stick the star to the floor. Whether you choose the square, the circle, or the oblong game-floor configuration, you'll have equal play sections, clear boundaries, and instant start and finish lines. And the best part? You can slide your furniture back over the game floor without disturbing it so it's ready the next time you're feeling playful. Now, let it rain, let it pour—indoor games are fun galore!

INDOOR GAME TIPS

✔ If you choose the square game-floor setup, use a different color of vinyl tape (electrical tape) for each side of the game floor. Otherwise, use different colors of tape to mark the inside Xs of the circle or oblong game floors. It's colorful and will give you more flexibility in having kids line up on specific colors to play games.

✔ Remind kids that voices need to be kept to a moderate level indoors. Also, lay down a rule of no thrown balls above the waist at any time!

✔ Encourage kids to use playing items from the Game Kit and the indoor game floor to invent their own new games and relays. Write down the rules and photocopy them for kids to take home. Be sure to staple or clip a copy to the back of this book for future playtimes.

PASS IT ON!

Mark 16:15; Acts 28:31

ENERGY LEVEL: Low
PLAYING TIME 10 minutes

GOAL OF THE GAME: Race items around the circle and be the first to have your item return to you.

Prior to playing, choose a different playing piece from the Game Kit for each child. For example if you have ten players, you'd need ten items, such as a beanbag sock, a scarf, a plastic plate, an inflated balloon, a rolling cube, a paper plate, a cotton ball, an index card, a table-tennis ball, and a paint stir stick. Place the items in the center of the floor and invite kids each to choose a playing piece. Have kids sit side by side in a large circle.

PLAYING PIECES

❏ Bible
❏ assorted Game Kit items, one for each child

LET'S PLAY!

Say: **Do you feel like racing today? Races are exciting because you're working against time and have to hurry to reach your goal. In this game, the goal is to pass items back and forth around and across the circle and to be the first to receive your racer back again. But to make our race even more exciting, I'll call out directions for you to follow, such as "Reverse directions," "Pass slowly," "Freeze," and "Pass across the circle." When I tell you to pass the item across the circle, stand up and walk the racer you're holding across to someone on the opposite side, then return to your place to begin racing again. We'll set the timer for three minutes and see if anyone's racer returns in that time. If your racer returns to you, hop up and call out "Goal!"**

Set the stopwatch or timer for three minutes, then begin the race by saying, "Pass to the right." Continue with the following racing directions:

✔ *Pass left.*
✔ *Speed up the passing.*
✔ *Freeze!* (Pause.) *Now pass across the circle.*

11

✔ *Reverse directions.*

✔ *Freeze.* (Pause.) *Now pass in any direction you'd like.*

Continue giving directions every fifteen seconds or so until someone calls out "Goal!" or time runs out. Then say: **That was a real race! Before we go for a few more laps, let's take a breather and see how racing our playing pieces is like racing to get the Good News about Jesus to others.**

PEP TALK

Have kids set their racers in the center of the circle. Then read aloud Mark 16:15 and Acts 28:31. Ask:

✔ *Why is it important to tell others about Jesus and his loving forgiveness?*

✔ *What things can we tell others about Jesus?*

✔ *Where can we go to tell people the Good News about Jesus?*

✔ *Why is it important to get the news about Jesus to others so quickly?*

✔ *In what ways do we sometimes have to change directions in telling others about Jesus?*

Lead kids to realize that sometimes when we try to tell others about Jesus they don't want to hear, so we may need to find other ways to express Jesus' love to them, such as through our actions.

Say: **We want everyone to know who Jesus is and what he has done for us. It's really like a race to tell them as quickly as possible so they can begin loving and following Jesus, too. Jesus guides and helps us in every way, and Jesus wants everyone to know he offers us love, forgiveness, and eternal life. Now let's choose new racers and race again. This time, however, we'll race until everyone's racer returns. When your racer returns, hop up and shout, "We're winners with Jesus!"**

READY, SET, GO!

2 Timothy 2:21; 4:2

ENERGY LEVEL: High
PLAYING TIME: 10 minutes

GOAL OF THE GAME: When your number is called, be the first to rush to the center and hold up the playing piece.

Prior to playing, lay the playing item on the center star (see page 8 for game-floor setups). Form four groups and have each group sit or stand along the outside edge of one section of the indoor game floor. Number each group from one to six. (If you have more than six kids to a side, repeat the numbers. It's okay to have two of each number per group.) Tell kids to remember their numbers. Hold the rolling cube.

LET'S PLAY!

Say: **I prepared for this game by setting up the indoor game floor and by setting a playing piece on the center star. And we've prepared by numbering off. I think we're ready to play! But first, how does it help to be prepared when we want to play a game?** Allow kids to respond, then continue: **Being prepared is important in a lot of things, and it will also help you play our game of Ready, Set, Go! In this game, I'll roll the rolling cube and call out the number rolled. If it's your number, hop to the center and quickly pick up the playing piece. If you're the first to pick it up, you can be the next to toss the rolling cube and call out the number. Now let's play!**

Begin playing by tossing the rolling cube and calling out the number rolled. You may wish to vary the way kids travel to the center star, such as walking backward, tiptoeing, and crawling. If you notice that one particular number isn't being rolled, call out that number before continuing play with the rolling cube. Continue until most of the kids (or all, if your class is small) have had a chance to be the caller.

Then say: **Wow! In this quick game, you have to be ready and willing to move. Let's take a break and see why it's important to be prepared Christians who are ready and willing to go for God.**

PLAYING TIPS

✔ *Vary the game a bit by assigning colors instead of numbers for the second round of play. Use the rolling cube to call out the colors rolled. Or for older kids, use colors AND numbers!*

PEP TALK

Read aloud 2 Timothy 2:21 and 4:2. Then ask:
✔ **What does being "prepared" mean?**

✔ *Why do you think we should be ready and willing to do God's work? to use and speak God's Word? to tell others about Jesus?*

✔ *What can we do now to be ready and prepared to serve God?* (Help kids realize that we can prepare by reading the Bible, praying, learning about Jesus, and being kind to others.)

Say: **Being ready and willing to serve God and speak his Word is important. And the only way to be ready is to prepare ourselves through learning about God and his Word. If I hadn't prepared for us to play a game, we couldn't have played. If we don't prepare to serve God or are not ready and willing to go when he calls us, we'll never get the job done! Let's play our game again, and this time if you snatch the playing piece, say "Ready, willing, and able!"**

GOOFY GOLF

Matthew 4:19; Romans 15:5, 6; 1 Corinthians 11:1

ENERGY LEVEL: Medium to high
PLAYING TIME: 15 minutes

GOAL OF THE GAME: Help your group make it around the course in as few strokes as possible.

Prior to playing, use masking tape or colored vinyl tape to set up a course outline on the floor as in the diagram on page 15. Use tape to make numbers from 1 to 8 on the tumblers. Place the tumblers on their sides on the course according to the dots in the diagram. Have kids form four golfing groups and hand each group a paint stir stick, an index card, a crayon, and a table-tennis ball. (Use cotton balls, if your kids are very young). Be sure you've numbered the table-tennis balls according to the directions on page 6.

LET'S PLAY!

Say: **Ah, it's a great day for a game of Goofy Golf, and we're all ready to play. This golf game is a**

PLAYING PIECES

❏ Bible
❏ 8 plastic tumblers
❏ 4 paint stir sticks
❏ 4 table-tennis balls
❏ 4 index cards
❏ crayons
❏ masking tape

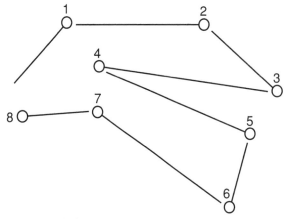

bit different from some of the golfing games you might have played. In this game, your whole team will be working to get your golf balls into the holes in the least number of strokes. Choose someone on your team to be the scorecard keeper and have that person number the card from one to eight. Pause while kids number their cards.

Continue: **Begin at any hole and take turns putting your golf ball toward the cup at the end of the tape line. Be sure to alternate putts with the other people in your group, then write your score for each hole on the scorecard. Play until your team has finished every hole on the course. When all the golfing groups are done, we'll add up the scores.**

After teams have completed all eight holes, compare the scores. Then say: **Give everyone in your golfing group high fives for completing the course! In the game of golf, we have to take careful aim and stay on the right course toward the target. Following Jesus helps us keep perfect aim in life, too! Let's take a quick breather and see how following Jesus keeps us on course and moving toward our heavenly target, God.**

PEP TALK

Read aloud Matthew 4:19; Romans 15:5, 6; and 1 Corinthians 11:1. Then ask:

✔ *In what ways does following Jesus help us stay on the right course to God?*

✔ *How does staying on course and moving closer to God help us each day?*

✔ *What are good ways to stay on course as we follow Jesus?*

Say: **When we carefully follow Jesus by obeying him, reading the Bible, being kind to others, and praying, we know that we are on the right course! Now let's get back to our golf course and play one more round of Goofy Golf before we end with another team high five.**

BELLY LAUGHS

1 Thessalonians 5:11; 3 John 8

ENERGY LEVEL: Medium to high
PLAYING TIME: 15 minutes

GOAL OF THE GAME: Be the first team to collect all of your playing items and bring them "home."

Prior to playing, clear a large playing area. Have kids form four teams and stand at one end of the playing area. Place the playing items in four piles at the opposite end of the room, making sure each pile has the same number of items. Have one person on each team blow up and tie off a balloon.

PLAYING PIECES

❑ Bible
❑ balloons
❑ a variety of playing pieces from the Game Kit

LET'S PLAY!

Say: **In this lively relay, you'll need some real teamwork and cooperation! The object of the relay is to travel with a partner to your team's pile of items and bring back items to place beside your team's line. And how will partners travel? With balloons held between their tummies! Be sure everyone on your team has at least one turn to travel. When all your items have been collected, have your team sit in place and shout, "Teamwork does it!"**

When every team is seated, say: **Teamwork sure got the job done, didn't it? Every team has its items back home, and everyone had a good time, too. Give your team members big high fives for your great teamwork. After the high fives, say: There's a lot to be said about working together and sharing the load. So let's take a breather as we see what the Bible says about teamwork.**

PEP TALK

Read aloud 1 Thessalonians 5:11 and 3 John 8. Then ask:
✔ *Why does teamwork help us? help others?*

16

✔ *How can teamwork be an encouragement?*

✔ *In what ways are we in a team with Christ? with fellow Christians?*

✔ *What things can be accomplished when we have teamwork with others and with Jesus?*

Say: **Teamwork works! When we help one another and encourage each other, great things can be accomplished. Let's give each other a team high five, then work to accomplish our relay once more.**

MATCH-UP

Psalm 119:125; Daniel 2:21; Matthew 12:33

ENERGY LEVEL: Low

PLAYING TIME: 15 minutes

GOAL OF THE GAME: Recognize who has chosen the same item as you through hearing descriptions of that item.

Prior to playing, make sure you have one item for each child. Have kids choose items, then find a place in the room to sit. Tell kids to keep their playing pieces hidden.

PLAYING PIECES

❑ Bible

❑ multiples of items, such as a pair of cotton balls, four plastic cups, three plastic plates, and two beanbag socks

LET'S PLAY!

When everyone has an item, say: **In this game you have to listen closely to descriptions and compare and contrast the descriptions with the item you've chosen. You'll hear three descriptions that will help you recognize if the item being described is the same playing piece you're holding. If you think you have the same item, stand up—but keep your item hidden until you're asked to reveal your playing piece.**

To begin, choose a child to describe her playing piece with three descriptive statements. For example, someone with a paper plate might say, "My item flies through the air," "It can be used to eat on," and "The item is flat and round." When kids are standing, have the child giving the description ask each child to reveal his playing piece and see if it's a match-up. Then have another volunteer give descriptions of her item. Continue until all the playing pieces have been identified.

Say: **You were good detectives in this game! You identified the descriptions carefully and considered whether you had a match. Choosing between right and wrong is much the same. Let's take a rest and see why it's important to make right choices by being good detectives and matching our choices to what God desires.**

PEP TALK

Read aloud Psalm 119:125; Daniel 2:21b; and Matthew 12:33. Then say: **When we look and listen closely to clues about choices we need to make, that's called "discernment." God helps us recognize good and bad aspects about choices so we can recognize which are the right choices to make.** Ask:

✔ *When has discernment helped you make a good choice?*
✔ *How can discernment keep us from getting into trouble? help us make good choices for God?*
✔ *In what ways can we help our discernment grow?*

Say: **Discernment is something we want to have a lot of, and we can help it grow by asking for God's help, through reading the Bible, by praying, and by wisely and carefully looking, listening, and thinking! Let's mix up the playing pieces and choose new ones. This time we'll only give two clues to help you discern if the item being described is the new item you've chosen!**

Play another round, then see if kids can guess the items with just one clue. For a variation, give descriptions of items in the classroom to see if kids can identify them.

FLIP-N-FLAP

Psalm 139:1-6

ENERGY LEVEL: Medium
PLAYING TIME: 10 minutes

GOAL OF THE GAME: Call out the names of people sitting on either side of you before the time is up.

Prior to playing, have kids sit in a large circle. Place the beach ball and the stopwatch or timer in the center of the circle.

LET'S PLAY!

Say: **Let's play a lively game called Flip-n-Flap to help you really learn each other's names. Turn to the people on your left and right and ask them their names right now. Don't forget which person is on the left and which is on the right!** (If your kids are young, this is a great game to help them identify right and left directions, in addition to learning the names of new friends.)

After kids have told each other their names, say: **I'll begin by tossing the ball to someone in the circle and calling out either "flip" or "flap." If I call out "flip," the person catching the ball must quickly tell me the name of the person to his left. And if I call out "flap," call out the name of the person to your right. If you get the name correct, you can be the next ball tosser. When I call out "mix 'em up," change places with someone in the circle, but you'll only have ten seconds to find a place!**

Use the stopwatch to time the ten seconds or count the seconds verbally. After kids change places, remind them to tell each other their names before beginning play again.

Continue playing until everyone has had a chance to be the ball tosser. Then say: **Wow! I think we all know each other's names by now, don't you? It would be impossible for us to learn the names of all the people in the world, but there is someone who knows each one. Let's discover who knows everyone's name and why knowing each other's names is helpful.**

PLAYING PIECES

❏ Bible
❏ stopwatch or timer
❏ beach ball

PLAYING TIPS

✔ *For a cool icebreaker, have kids learn favorite foods, colors, and pets' names from their neighbors, in addition to their names.*

PEP TALK

Read aloud Psalm 139:1-6. Then ask:
  ✔ **Who knows all our names and everyone's name in the world?**
  ✔ **What else does God know about us?**

✔ *How does knowing our names demonstrate God's love for us?*

✔ *In what ways can knowing each other's names be helpful? increase our communication? encourage us to be friendlier?*

Say: **God knows not only my name, but he also knows me—and that makes me feel loved. We can show others we care about them when we take the time to learn their names. Let's play again, but this time repeat the first and last names of the people on either side of you. If we can name everyone's name, we'll end with friendly high fives.**

WALK THE LINE

Matthew 7:1, 2; Romans 2:1

ENERGY LEVEL: Medium
PLAYING TIME: 10 minutes

GOAL OF THE GAME: See if you can travel down a straight line without losing your balance.

Prior to playing, stick two 8- to 10-foot masking-tape lines to the floor, parallel and about 2 feet apart. Put the lines in a clear area, away from tables, chairs, or sharp corners.

LET'S PLAY!

Have kids gather at one end of the tape lines, then say: **Here are two straight paths. In a moment, we'll see if you can walk the lines without falling off. But first, raise your hand if you think**

PLAYING PIECES

❏ Bible
❏ masking tape

this could be a challenging game; if you think it will be too simple, show thumbs down.

Allow time for kids to respond, then ask for two volunteers and have them each stand at one end of the tape lines. Say: **Before you walk our paths, let's put a spin on the game!** Twirl the two kids around several times, then let them walk the lines. Be prepared for gales of giggles as kids wobble and wiggle their way down the paths.

Continue having kids twirl and tromp the paths until everyone has had a turn. Then have kids sit down. Ask:

✔ *What did you first think when you thought we were just going to walk a simple line?*

✔ *What do you think of our dizzy game now?*

✔ *How was judging this game before playing it like judging people without first knowing them?*

Say: **You know, even though we may have judged our game boring before we played, it turned out to be lots of fun with loads of laughter. Now let's see what the Bible says about judging people.**

PEP TALK

Ask volunteers to read aloud Matthew 7:1, 2 and Romans 2:1. Ask:

✔ *Why is it important not to judge others?*

✔ *How is judging others before knowing them unfair?*

Say: **Jesus taught us not to be judgmental of others, or else we will be judged. Jesus wants us to get to know others by being kind to them, by caring for and sharing with them. You have probably heard the saying that we shouldn't judge a book by its cover.** Ask:

✔ *What do you think that saying means?*

✔ *How is this saying true for judging people by the way they look or talk?*

Say: **Jesus warns us against judging others, and that's an important lesson to remember. Just like in our game, we need to give people a chance and not jump to wrong conclusions about them. Jesus accepted people without judging them, and that's what we want to do, too. We judged our game as too simple before we had a chance to play. But once we played, we realized what a fun challenge it was. Now let's have a bit more fun and walk that line again. But this time you can choose whether to walk, hop, crawl, or tiptoe down the line.**

DODGE-PODGE

Matthew 26:41; Luke 11:4; 1 Corinthians 10:13

ENERGY LEVEL: High
PLAYING TIME: 15 minutes

GOAL OF THE GAME: Dodge the ball and be the last team in the game.

Prior to playing, be sure an indoor game floor is set up. Help kids number off by fours and have each group of numbers stand in one of the four sections of the game floor.

LET'S PLAY!

Hold the beach ball and say: **In dodge ball, you have to be fast in order to dodge being tagged by the ball. It takes quick thinking, fast reactions, and lots of dodging. Let's play a game of Dodge-Podge. We'll play the game like dodge ball, but in this version you must stay in your section of the game floor or you're out. If you catch the ball and don't drop it, you can be the next one to throw the ball. But if you get tagged by the ball or drop it, you can stand behind your group and cheer them on to victory!**

Play the game as regular dodge ball, tossing the ball back and forth between sides until there is only one team with one or more members remaining. Then say: **Whew! That was a lot of fast action and dodging! You know, we dodge a lot of things in life that might tempt us to say wrong things or to act in ways that are not pleasing to God. Let's see how God can help us dodge temptation and stay away from evil.**

PEP TALK

Invite several volunteers to read aloud Matthew 26:41; Luke 11:4; and 1 Corinthians 10:13. Then ask:

PLAYING PIECES

❏ Bible
❏ beach ball
❏ indoor game-floor setup (see page 8)

✔ *What are things God wants us to avoid?*

✔ *How do God and his Word help us dodge evil and resist temptations?*

✔ *In what ways can staying close to God help us steer clear of evil? say no to people and things that tempt us?*

Say: **Dodging evil and temptations in real life is not only important, it can also save our lives! Let's play another game of Dodge-Podge, but this time if you get tagged, say, "The Lord helps me!" and you can have another chance to stay in the game.** Play for several more minutes, then end the game and have kids give each other high fives.

PASS THE POLLEN

Matthew 5:44; 19:19; Romans 12:10

ENERGY LEVEL: Low to medium
PLAYING TIME: 10-15 minutes

GOAL OF THE GAME: Work with the group to pass balloons with your feet!

Prior to playing, inflate three or four balloons and knot the ends. Have kids form a large circle and lie on the floor so their heads point toward the center of the circle and their legs point outward.

PLAYING PIECES

❑ Bible
❑ 3-4 balloons

LET'S PLAY!

Say: **Wow! You look like a big flower with your feet and legs as the petals. In this game, we'll pass these pretend balls of pollen around the circle.** Hold up the balloons. **Since flowers don't have arms or hands, they must use their petals to catch and hold pollen—so we'll pass the balloon "pollen" using our feet! It's not as easy as it sounds, and you'll have to cooperate with each other to accomplish this amazing "feet"! We'll start several pieces of pollen around the circle and see if each piece makes it all the way around.**

When the balloons have gone around the circle, have kids sit up. Say: **That was fun to watch, but I'm sure it was not as easy as you made it look. Sometimes passing Jesus' love to others isn't as easy as it would seem, either. So let's take a breather and explore how we can pass Jesus' love to the people around us.**

PEP TALK

Read aloud Matthew 5:44; 19:19; and Romans 12:10. Ask:

✔ *When is it easy to love others? When is it difficult?*
✔ *Why do you think it's hard to love everyone all the same?*
✔ *Why do you think Jesus wants us to pass his love to everyone, even our enemies?*
✔ *How can we pass Jesus' love to those who love us? to those who may not love us in return?*

Say: **Jesus wants us to love everyone—even those who may not seem very lovable. Sometimes that's hard. People who have different beliefs than we do or treat us unkindly make it hard to act loving. But because we love Jesus, he passes to us an extra dose of love and patience that helps us be kind to others and help them, even if they seem unlovable. When we know we're loved by Jesus, we're ready to pass his love on to others. Let's play Pass the Pollen once more, except this time as you pass it on, say "Pass Jesus' love to others!"**

DODGE BOWLING
Proverbs 4:14, 15; Matthew 4:3, 4; 26:41; 1 Thessalonians 5:22

ENERGY LEVEL: Medium
PLAYING TIME: 15 minutes

GOAL OF THE GAME: Bowl over the opponents' pins before being tagged.

Prior to playing, set up one of the indoor game floors from page 8. Direct kids to form two teams and have each team stand on one half of the game floor. Hand each team four plastic tumblers, then instruct teams to set the tumblers up around their playing sections.

LET'S PLAY!

Say: **Let's play a crazy game of indoor bowling in which you not only try to bowl down the tumbler pins but also have to dodge the bowling ball! We'll use this beach ball as a bowling ball. The object of Dodge Bowling is to knock over your opponents' pins while protecting your own pins and not being tagged by the ball. If you're tagged, you must sit around the outside of the game floor and help toss the ball back into the game if it escapes. We'll play until one team has either knocked over all their opponents' pins or tagged all their players out.**

PLAYING PIECES

❑ Bible
❑ 8 plastic tumblers
❑ beach ball
❑ indoor game-floor setup

After the game is over, say: **That was some great dodging! I'm sure you would like a rematch, and we'll have one in a moment. But first, let's see how God helps us dodge temptations that try to tag us out in real life.**

PEP TALK

Invite volunteers to read aloud Proverbs 4:14, 15; Matthew 4:3, 4; 26:41; and 1 Thessalonians 5:22. Then ask:

✔ *How did Jesus dodge and say no to Satan's temptations?*
✔ *What are some temptations we need to dodge and say no to?*
✔ *How can learning God's Word help us avoid temptations? How can prayer help us?*

Say: **There are many bad and evil things we as Christians want to avoid, such as lying, cheating, being with bad friends, and treating others with meanness and disrespect. God helps strengthen us against these kinds of temptations just as he strengthened Jesus. Jesus knew that learning God's Word, then using it to say no to temptations is one good way God helps us. Prayer is another way God helps us avoid temptation. And when we work to dodge and avoid temptations, we're showing God how much we trust and respect him. Let's play Dodge Bowling once more. Each time you dodge the ball, name one temptation we can dodge through God's help. Then we'll end with a prayer thanking God for his powerful help!**

After playing one more time, pray: **Dear God, thank you for helping give us strength to recognize and say no to evil and to temptations that threaten to draw us away from you. Help us be strong in Jesus' name. Amen.**

UMBRELLA SMOOSH

Romans 15:7; Philippians 2:29

ENERGY LEVEL: High
PLAYING TIME: 10 minutes

GOAL OF THE GAME: Rush to form groups with the correct number of members.

Prior to playing, clear a large playing area and collect the rolling cube. You'll also need a paper plate for each child. Have kids gather at one end of the room.

PLAYING PIECES

❑ Bible
❑ paper plates
❑ rolling cube
(see page 6)

LET'S PLAY!

Hand each child a paper plate. Say: **Have you ever rushed to join someone under an umbrella in the pouring rain? It can get crowded under an umbrella! Let's play a funny game of Umbrella Smoosh. In this game, I'll toss the rolling cube and call out the number rolled. You must all rush to form groups of that number and hold your paper-plate umbrellas over your heads. Anyone left out of an umbrella group can count the people in each group to be sure they have the correct number. Then I'll roll the cube again.**

Play several rounds and let kids rush to form their umbrella groups. Then say: **It's a good thing it's not raining, or most of us would be wet by now! How did you feel if you were left out of an umbrella group?** Encourage kids to share their feelings, then say: **Being left out in real-life situations isn't a happy feeling, is it? So let's take a break and discover why it's important to include and welcome others as friends.**

PEP TALK

Read aloud Romans 15:7 and Philippians 2:29. Ask:
✔ *Why do you think Jesus wants us to accept others?*
✔ *How does welcoming people to our circle of friends, to church, or in*

our classes at school show our love for Jesus? for others?

✔ **In what ways does including others help them feel accepted and loved? Why is this important?**

✔ **In what ways can you include others in church? in school? in your neighborhood?**

Say: **Jesus wants us to accept others and be kind to them. When we draw others closer to us, we draw closer to**  **Jesus! Plus, including others who might be left out helps them feel accepted and valued—and it shows that we respect and care for them, just as Jesus does. We'll play Umbrella Smoosh once more, but this time, if someone is left out of an umbrella group, invite him to join yours!**

TIGHTROPE TIPTOE

Proverbs 2:6; 19:11

ENERGY LEVEL: Low to medium
PLAYING TIME: 15 minutes

GOAL OF THE GAME: Devise ways to get around, over, or past other players standing on the game square within the time limit.

If you haven't already done so, lay out an indoor game floor according to the directions on page 8. Place the beanbag sock on the center star. Have kids form four teams and line up outside the edges of the game floor, one team per section. Players will be walking along the outer edge of the game floor, so be sure team members are standing behind the tape lines so they don't block players' paths.

PLAYING PIECES

❑ Bible
❑ stopwatch or timer
❑ beanbag sock

LET'S PLAY!

Say: **Are you ready to solve a few problems and have a ton of fun, too? Then let's get set to play Tightrope Tiptoe. In this game, you'll be tiptoeing around all four sections of the game floor, then along one of the diagonal lines to snatch the beanbag. Sound easy? Well, there is one problem. Other people will also be tiptoeing in different directions around the edge! You'll need to figure out how to politely pass each other while staying on the line. If you fall off, you can go to the center and cheer your next team members on.**

Explain that two people from each team will begin to travel the outline in opposite directions (a total of eight kids will be moving along the outline at the same time). When each child has traveled around all four sides of the game floor, she can travel along one of the diagonal lines to snatch the beanbag. Score one point for the team who snatches the beanbag, then begin again with eight new players. Continue until all players have traveled around the game floor.

When everyone has tiptoed on the tightrope, say: **Whew! There were some big traffic jams. How did you solve your traffic troubles?** Let kids describe their solutions, then say: **It often feels like we're walking a tightrope with all of life's problems, doesn't it? And we need special wisdom and patience to solve those problems so we can get past them. Let's sit on our tightrope for a moment as we discover the best ways to solve life's problems.**

PLAYING TIPS

✔ *For a real challenge, have older kids all walk the tightrope at once, with teams going in opposite directions, by walking backward or traveling in pairs!*

PEP TALK

Ask volunteers to read aloud Proverbs 2:6 and 19:11. Then ask:
- ✔ *How can God and his Word help us solve problems in our lives?*
- ✔ *Why is asking God's help in solving problems a wise thing to do?*
- ✔ *In what ways does God's Word help us solve problems? How does faith help?*

Say: **God and his Word offer us the wisdom, patience, and power we need to deal with any problem in our lives—if we simply trust God and have faith in God's Word. Let's play Tightrope Tiptoe once more to remind us how we can get past problems on life's tightrope with God's help.**

STRETCH-N-REACH

Galatians 5:22, 23; 1 Timothy 4:9, 10

ENERGY LEVEL: High
PLAYING TIME: 15 minutes

GOAL OF THE GAME: Be the first tugging team to reach your playing piece.

Prior to playing, be sure the indoor game-floor con-figuration is set up on the floor (see page 8). Help kids line up and number off by fours. Have each team stand near an outside corner of the game floor. Place one playing item each at opposite ends of any diago-nal line on the game-floor diagram. The rope will be tugged along this diagonal line as kids try to reach the item on their side. (If teams are large, back up the items to the corners of your classroom.)

PLAYING PIECES

❏ Bible
❏ long jump rope
❏ two playing pieces from the Game Kit
❏ indoor game floor

LET'S PLAY!

Say: **Are you ready to reach and stretch those muscles today? Well, let's play a tugging game to see if you can be the first team to stretch out and reach your playing item. We'll play with two teams and have each hold one section of this rope, with the first players in line stepping on the center star to begin the tug. When I call "tug away!" each team will pull backward toward its item. The first team to stretch and reach its item plays the next team.**

Continue playing until each team has had a turn. Then say: **You had quite a reach to complete these tugs, didn't you? So shake out your arms and take a breather as we learn how we need to stretch and reach to be better Christians.**

PEP TALK

Say: **Being powerful Christians isn't always easy. Let's read about the values we need to stretch and reach for to become the kind of Christians**

Jesus wants us to be. Read aloud Galatians 5:22, 23 and 1 Timothy 4:9, 10, then ask:

✔ *What qualities do we need to reach and strive for in our lives?*
✔ *How can having these values help us become more powerful Christians? draw us nearer to Jesus? to others?*
✔ *What can we do to develop these values? How does God help us?*

Say: **Jesus wants us to stretch and reach for these good values even though it's not always easy. Seeing how Jesus treated others and how he took time to learn God's Word can help us do the same. We can nurture positive values such as patience, kindness, forgiveness, and honesty. This time when we tug, think of those positive values and, when you reach your item, shout, "Values are worth the work!" then name a value Jesus wants us to reach for.**

PLAYING TIPS

✔ *If you have a second tugging rope, have four teams tug in a crisscross pattern by placing one rope over the other.*

TOSS 'EM ACROSS

Deuteronomy 7:6; 1 Peter 2:9

ENERGY LEVEL: Medium to low
PLAYING TIME: 15 minutes

GOAL OF THE GAME: Keep tossing the ball in a pattern as you add kids to the circle.

Prior to playing, be sure you have the indoor game floor set up. Have kids stand around the edges of the room.

LET'S PLAY!

Stand on the outline of the game floor holding the beach ball. Say: **Let's play a lively toss-n-catch game in which you need to remember the pattern that the ball is tossed. I'll invite someone to join me across the game floor, and we'll toss the ball back**

PLAYING PIECES

❑ Bible
❑ beach ball
❑ indoor game-floor setup

30

and forth two times. Then the person I invited will ask someone else to join us, and that person will be added to our tossing pattern. We'll toss the ball in our new pattern for two complete tossing cycles. We'll keep inviting new players to join us and to toss the ball in our constantly growing pattern until everyone is included in the game.

Begin by asking another child to stand on the game outline opposite you. Toss the ball back and forth two times, then invite another player to join. Each time someone new joins, have that person toss you the ball as you begin your tossing sequence again. When the entire class is in the game, continue your tossing pattern for two more complete cycles.

Then say: **This is fun! We began with just me, but now a whole lot of friends have joined in to play! That's how it is when God calls us to be part of his family. He calls us one by one, and we join God's family to do so many things together. Let's sit in place for a moment as we discover what being part of God's family is all about and what things we can do together as a family.**

PLAYING TIPS

✔ *Play this game at the beginning of the year as a classroom icebreaker and to help everyone get acquainted. You may wish to have kids call out each other's names each time they toss the ball to someone.*

PEP TALK

Read aloud Deuteronomy 7:6 and 1 Peter 2:9. Then ask:

✔ *Who is in God's family?*

✔ *Why is it so wonderful to join God's special family?*

✔ *How do we help each other as members of God's family?*

Say: **Being called to join God's family is so wonderful! It means we can show God and others how much we love the Lord and care for one another. When we are part of God's family, we worship together, we pray together, we help one another, and we grow closer to God and to each other. Just think how lonely it would be not to join in! That's why God wants us to encourage others to be part of the family. We can do this by telling others about the Lord and his great love and by showing that God's people treat others kindly. Wouldn't it be awesome if *everyone* wanted to be part of God's special family? Let's play our join-in game once more to remind us how great it feels to be called to join in the fun of God's family!**

LOST LAMB

John 10:4, 5, 14, 27, 28

ENERGY LEVEL: Low
PLAYING TIME: 15 minutes

GOAL OF THE GAME: Be the first player to locate the lost sheep using verbal directions from your team.

Prior to playing, set up one of the indoor game floors on page 8. Have kids form four groups, then have each group stand by a different portion of the game floor. Set the beanbag sock inside the boundaries of the game floor. Young children especially like this hunt-n-find game.

PLAYING PIECES

❏ Bible
❏ 1 beanbag sock
❏ stopwatch or timer
❏ indoor game floor

LET'S PLAY!

Say: **Let's play a hunt-and-find game called Lost Lamb. One player from each team will come inside the boundaries and close his eyes. No peeking, because that will take all the fun out of this game! I'll quietly hide the beanbag "lamb" somewhere within the game-floor boundaries and then set the timer for three minutes. When I say "Go!" the players inside the game area will crawl across the floor to try and find the lost lamb. Your teammates will be pretend shepherds who help by giving you directions like "go to the left" or "turn around." You'll have to listen carefully to your shepherds to hear their directions! When the lamb is found, we'll choose four new players to hunt for the lost lamb.**

If your group is large, let two or three kids from each team hunt for the lost sheep at one time. Play several rounds of the game, then say: **This game takes some careful listening, doesn't it? We have to listen carefully to the voice of our own shepherd. Let's take a break and learn who our Good Shepherd is and why it's important to listen to him.**

PEP TALK

Ask volunteers to read aloud John 10:4, 5, 14, 27, 28. Then ask:

✔ *Who is our Good Shepherd? Why is Jesus called the Good Shepherd?*

✔ *Why is it important to listen carefully to Jesus? to follow what he says?*

✔ *How can we learn more about what Jesus tells us?*

Say: **Jesus is called our Good Shepherd because he loves and cares for us as a shepherd cares for his sheep. And we recognize Jesus' words by his love, truth, and wisdom. We're like sheep in Jesus' flock—we want to stay near to hear his voice and do exactly what he says. When we listen to and obey Jesus' voice, he will help lead us through troubles and show us the way to God. I'm so glad that Jesus is my Good Shepherd and the voice I want to always trust and obey! Let's play Lost Lamb a few more times. This time when you find the lost lamb, say, "We know our shepherd's voice!"**

HOLD ON!

Deuteronomy 6:6-9; Psalm 119:11, 105

ENERGY LEVEL: Medium to high

PLAYING TIME: 10-15 minutes

GOAL OF THE GAME: Make it through the obstacle course without dropping the plates.

Prior to playing, place two zigzag rows of plastic tumblers across the length of the playing area, four tumblers to a row. Form two teams and hand each team a plastic plate. Have teams line up at one end of the playing area and tell the first players in line to set the plastic plates on their heads.

PLAYING PIECES

❏ Bible

❏ 8 plastic tumblers

❏ 2 plastic plates

LET'S PLAY!

Say: **Are you ready for a zany relay race? In this wild relay, you'll need a great sense of balance to make it through our obstacle course. When I** say "Go!" the first players in each line will zigzag around the cups in their row while balancing the plastic plates on their heads, without using hands. When players reach the end of the cups, they must keep going and zigzag their way back to the line. If you drop a plate at any time, you must take three steps backward, then replace the plate and continue from there. Let's see which team can make it through the obstacle course and back in the shortest time.

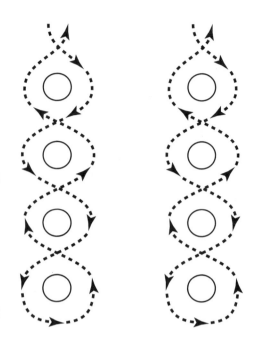

Begin the relay and encourage kids to cheer for their teammates. When both teams have completed the race, have kids sit in place. Say: **Whew! That was a real balancing act, wasn't it? Sometimes it almost seemed that everyone was moving backward—but little by little you made it through the obstacle course. Let's run the relay once more, but this time we'll hold the plates to our hearts instead of balancing them on our heads. Do you think it will be an easier relay? We'll, let's see!**

Run the relay again, this time letting kids clutch the plates to their chests. There shouldn't be many "drops" this time! When both teams are finished, say: **That was a much quicker race! Why was it easier for you?** Allow time for kids to respond, then continue: **When we hold things very near and close to us, they're more secure and stable. It's exactly the same with holding God's Word close to our hearts. Let's take a quick break and discover how holding and keeping God's Word close to us helps us make it through obstacles in real life.**

PEP TALK

Invite volunteers to read aloud Deuteronomy 6:6-9 and Psalm 119:11, 105. Then ask:

✔ *Why is it important to learn and use God's Word every day?*
✔ *How does God's Word help us if we keep it near our hearts and minds?*
✔ *In what ways can we keep God's Word locked in our hearts and minds?*

Say: **Just knowing sort of what God's Word says is like balancing a plate on our heads. It doesn't have a solid base to rest on, and we may lose** it along the way. But keeping God's Word close to our hearts and minds makes it secure inside us and ready to help us as we go through life. Let's form new teams and play once more holding the plates close to us as we go through the obstacles. Then we'll end with a prayer thanking God for helping us to learn and keep his Word close to our hearts.

After the race, pray: **Dear God, there's nothing more powerful, beautiful, and important than your Word. Please help us work to learn your Word, then always hold your Word close to our hearts and minds. Amen.**

GREAT EXCHANGE

Psalm 55:19; Matthew 18:3; Ephesians 4:22-24

ENERGY LEVEL: Medium to high
PLAYING TIME: 15 minutes

GOAL OF THE GAME: Rush to find the correct place to stand according to your number.

Prior to playing, have kids form a large circle and hand each child a paper plate. Number off around the circle from one to six and have each child write her number on a paper plate. Instruct kids to mix up and form another large circle, then tape their plates to the floor where they're standing, so you have a large circle of mixed numbered plates (see page 36). Tell kids to stand on a plate with their number.

PLAYING PIECES

❑ Bible
❑ paper plates
❑ masking tape
❑ crayons
❑ rolling cube
  (see page 6)

LET'S PLAY!

Say: **Are you ready for a little bit of switch-o, change-o fun? In this game, called Great Exchange, you'll walk around the circle, stepping from plate to plate as you follow my directions. But when I shout, "The great exchange!" rush to stand on a plate with your number. The last one to reach his plate can roll the cube during the next round.**

Begin by rolling the cube and giving a direction corresponding to the rolled number, such as "three steps forward" or "six steps backward." After the first "great exchange," have the last child to reach a plate roll the cube to determine the next number of moves. Continue playing until most kids have had a turn to be the roller.

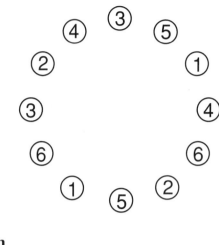

Then say: **Wow! That was a lively game, wasn't it? You had to be ready to exchange places quickly in Great Exchange. In the same way, we have to be willing to change places for God, too. Let's take a break and learn how God calls us to change if we're in the wrong places.**

PEP TALK

Read aloud Psalm 55:19; Matthew 18:3; and Ephesians 4:22-24. Then say: **Sometimes we find ourselves in a place that God might not approve of or be happy about. Those are times when we need to change places and get to the place God wants us to be. For example, we might find ourselves hanging out with friends who aren't nice or make bad decisions. That's not a place God wants us to be, and we would need to change places right away to a healthier bunch of friends.** Ask:

✔ *Why does God care about the situations we're in?*

✔ *How does being willing to change places for God show him our love? our trust and faith?*

✔ *What makes it hard to change places? What can we do to help us change places when we need to?*

Say: **It's not always easy to change our attitudes or situations, but if they're not what God wants them to be, it's important to have the courage to change anyway! Knowing God's Word and praying are two powerful ways to find out where God wants us, and they can also help us change to the places God wants us to be. Let's play Great Exchange once more. This time, however, when you exchange places, give the players on either side of you a high five and say, "God wants us in good places!"**

Section 2:

OUTDOOR DASHES

- ☑ races and relays
- ☑ water fun
- ☑ team contests
- ☑ and more!

Red rover, red rover—send fun times right over!

You probably remember oodles of outdoor games from growing up, including Red Rover, Mother May I? and perhaps even Ante, Ante Over. The rules may have faded with time, but the memories of fun and friends haven't! There's nothing quite as exciting and inviting as outdoor races, relays, jump-rope jingles, team tag, and running games. But the games in "Outdoor Dashes" aren't your typical old-time favorites—they're bright and fresh for today's kids and include soon-to-be new favorites such as Airport, Clean the Attic, Interference, and Waterworks. And best of all: with the cool Game Kit you've prepared (see page 7), you can play these lively games anytime, anyplace. They're perfect for Sunday school, church picnics, vacation Bible school, and family retreats. Now get ready for some cool fun in the outdoor sun!

OUTDOOR GAME TIPS

✔ Choose play areas that are free of trees, bushes, shrubs, hidden stumps, and the congregation's favorite flower beds!

✔ Designate two kids to be the Game Kit Keepers for the day. These two helpers will make sure your Game Kit arrives in one piece outdoors and safely (and completely) back in the classroom when you're done playing.

✔ Consider purchasing an inexpensive whistle to blow during outdoor games. Use the whistle to signal start and stop times as well as time-outs just before Pep Talk discussions.

✔ Host an occasional "Guest Game Day" and invite another class to join your outdoor fun. Have your kids choose two games prior to the special day and be prepared to explain the playing directions to your visitors. Consider providing cool fruit juice and crackers during the Pep Talk time. End game time with lively high fives between the classes.

NOTE: Some of the games in this section require a bucket or pitcher and water, so be sure to check the Playing Pieces list before choosing a game.

AIRPORT

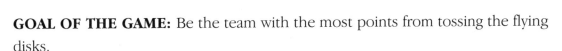

Matthew 28:19, 20; Hebrews 3:14; 10:36

ENERGY LEVEL: Medium to high
PLAYING TIME: 15 minute

GOAL OF THE GAME: Be the team with the most points from tossing the flying disks.

Prior to playing, place the paint sticks about 20 feet apart to make a semi square (see illustration on page 40). Place a large plastic plate by each paint stick. Have kids letter off from A to D and assign each team a different side of the square.

PLAYING PIECES

- ❏ Bible
- ❏ 4 paint stir sticks
- ❏ stopwatch or timer
- ❏ 4 large plastic plates

LET'S PLAY!

Shield your eyes and scan the sky. Then say: **What a great day to play Airport! In this high-flying game, you'll take turns flying our pretend plate airplanes toward other sides of the square. If your plane lands safely at another team's "airport," your team will score one point. But if your opponents catch the plane as it's trying to land, you score nothing, and that team can toss the plane to another airport. Remember to take turns and let everyone on your team be a pilot and have a turn flying the plane. We'll see how many smooth landings you can make in five minutes. Ready? Take off!**

After five minutes, close down the airports and say: **You made some good, solid landings, I see. Give your copilots high fives for their teamwork!** Pause for kids to respond, then ask:

✔ *How did patience and perseverance help in this game?*
✔ *What would have happened if you'd given up trying to land your pretend planes?*

Say: **To make a landing in our game, you had to keep trying over and over. It's much the same way when we're trying to land Jesus' love in someone's** heart. Sometimes we have to keep trying over and over to get the message across. So let's make a short layover and learn how patience and perseverance help us in sharing Jesus with others.

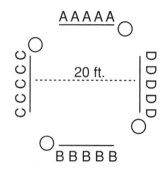

```
         AAAAA  ○
    ○
    C
○ C           D D D D D
  C  ┈┈┈ 20 ft. ┈┈┈
○ C           ○
  C
    ○
     B B B B B
```

PEP TALK

Read aloud Matthew 28:19, 20 and Hebrews 3:14; 10:36. Then ask:

✔ *What are things that might interfere or try to stop us from telling others about Jesus?*

✔ *In what ways does perseverance help us tell others about Jesus?*

✔ *How does telling others about Jesus help give them smooth landings in life?*

✔ *What are things we could tell someone about Jesus and his love for us?*

Say: **Jesus wants us to tell others about him, but sometimes that can be very frustrating. People may not want to listen or think they can get by without Jesus. We know that's not true and want to help them realize the truth. Even though it may be hard at times to tell others about Jesus and his love, the important thing is not to stop trying but to persevere until we land the message about Jesus' love in their hearts. Let's play another round of Airport. This time when you make a safe landing, shout, "I'll persevere for Jesus!"**

PLAYING TIPS

✔ *Play partner Airport by having one partner be the tosser and one the catcher. The fun twist? Partners must keep their elbows locked during play!*

FOXTAILS

Proverbs 4:14, 15; 1 Thessalonians 5:22; James 4:7, 8

ENERGY LEVEL: High
PLAYING TIME: 10 minutes

GOAL OF THE GAME: Don't let your team's foxtail be stolen!

Prior to playing, have kids form two teams and stand in lines holding each other's waists to make two long "foxes." Hand each fox a fabric square to tuck in the last player's waistband or belt as a foxtail.

PLAYING PIECES

❑ Bible
❑ 2 fabric squares

LET'S PLAY!

Say: **This game is called Foxtails. The object of the game is to snatch the foxtail away from the other fox. When a steal is made, a point is scored for that fox. If a fox comes "undone" while running, I'll call out "Fox trot!" Then both foxes must scramble up their member's positions to form new foxes with new players as the tails. We'll play until one fox team has scored three points.**

When one team has made three points, have the foxes sit down to rest. Say: **You looked so funny chasing your tails like puppies! It must have been hard to steer clear of your opponents as they tried to snatch away your tail! There are many temptations we want to steer clear of too—temptations that threaten to snatch us away from following and obeying God. We all know our opponent is called Satan. Now let's take a break and see how we can steer clear of our evil opponent's temptations!**

PEP TALK

Invite volunteers to read aloud Proverbs 4:14, 15; 1 Thessalonians 5:22; and James 4:7, 8. Then ask:

✔ ***What are some temptations we want to steer clear of?***
✔ ***Why do you think Satan sends temptations and bad things our way?***
✔ ***What do we need to do to resist temptations? What will God do for us?***

Say: **When we draw near to God, follow his Word, pray, and keep our eyes on Jesus, we have the power to steer clear of the temptations sent by our evil opponent! Just remember what James 4:7, 8 says: "Resist the devil, and he will flee from you. Come near to God, and he will come near to you"! Let's repeat those verses together.** Lead kids in repeating James 4:7, 8 two more times. Then say: **Now let's play Foxtails again to remind us how God helps us steer clear of temptations.**

PASS THE PICKLES

Ephesians 4:32; 1 Thessalonians 5:15

ENERGY LEVEL: High
PLAYING TIME: 10 minutes

GOAL OF THE GAME: Help your group relay "pickles" across the finish line.

Prior to playing, place two fabric squares side by side and approximately 5 feet apart. Place two more fabric squares 20 feet opposite the first ones. Have kids form two groups and line up behind the first fabric squares. Divide the playing items and place them by the last players in each line. If you have an uneven number of kids, one child will go twice in this relay.

PLAYING PIECES

❑ Bible
❑ 4 fabric squares
❑ 1 playing item for each child

LET'S PLAY!

Say: **How many of you like puckery pickles? Well, this game will give you a chance to pass pretend pickles as you race to get your pickles piled up at the opposite end of the field. Here's how this goofy game works: The last players in each line will kneel down, pick up a pretend pickle, and place it under their chins. Then those players will pass the pickles, chin-to-chin, to the next players in line and so on. When the first players in line receive the pickles, they must run with them to the fabric squares and drop them in a pile. After running back to the line, those players become the last people in line and start the next pickle pass! You can encourage your teammates with lots of cheers and clapping.**

Begin the relay and play until all pickles are collected at the opposite end of the playing area. Then say: **What expert pickle-passers you all are! And I liked how team members cheered for and encouraged one another, especially when it was hard to pass an item. Let's take a quick break and**

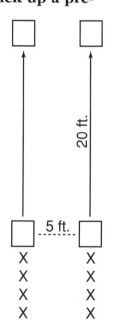

look at how we can pass kindness and encouragement to one another.

PEP TALK

Read aloud Ephesians 4:32 and 1 Thessalonians 5:15. Then ask:

✔ *Why do you think God wants us to pass along kindness?*

✔ *When is it difficult to pass on kindness? What can make it easier?*

✔ *How can being kind to someone encourage more kindness?*

✔ *In what ways can we pass kindness and encouragement on to others?*

Say: **Passing kindness, caring, love, encouragement, and help to others is like a relay. Those people feel good in return and want to pass along the kindness to even more people, who also continue relaying the kindness! Pretty neat, isn't it? Let's play Pass the Pickles again, but this time we'll form two new teams to play.**

GREETINGS!

Romans 16:16; Philippians 2:29; 3 John 14

ENERGY LEVEL: Medium
PLAYING TIME: 10 minutes

GOAL OF THE GAME: Be the first trio to greet one each other.

Prior to playing, form trios and have each trio stand in a line about 10 feet away from each other. Hand the first person in each line four crayons. Have kids slide the crayons between the fingers of their right hands, one crayon between every two fingers.

LET'S PLAY!

Ask kids to name ways people greet each other, such as through a "hello," a handshake, or even a hug.

PLAYING PIECES

❏ Bible
❏ package of crayons

Then say: **Are you ready to play a fast-paced game of Greetings? In this game, the first person in line will hop to the second person and greet that player with a hearty "hello." Then the players will shake hands and transfer the crayons to the second player's fingers without using their left hands. After the transfer, the second player will hop to the third person and greet and transfer the crayons. The third person will then return to the first player and say "hello" as they transfer crayons. When you're all done, sit in place quickly. If you drop a crayon along the way, pick it up and slide it back between your fingers before moving on.**

A ⋯5 ft.⋯ B   C   D

10 ft.

A   B   C   D

A   B   C   D

When all the trios are seated, say: **It was fun to watch everyone meeting and greeting one another. Saying hello to friends can be fun and make us feel good inside, too. Let's see if there's anything in the Bible that tells us about greeting one another and why it's important to be so friendly.**

PEP TALK

Ask several kids to read aloud Romans 16:16; Philippians 2:29; and 3 John 14. Then ask:

✔ *How did people in Bible days greet one another?*
✔ *How were their greetings like ours today? How were they different?*
✔ *Why is it important to greet and be friendly to one another?*

Say: **Greeting one another is not just a way of showing that we're friends; it's also a way of being encouraging, kind, and accepting because we recognize that we share a wonderful gift in Jesus! This week, let's all make it a point to meet and greet people we know and share a smile with them. Right now, let's form new trios and meet and greet more friends with a smile.**

PLAYING TIPS

✔ *This is a great ice-breaker for the start of the year and can be played indoors as well as out! Or have your kids greet adult worshipers with this fun idea and get the smiles going!*

INTERFERENCE

Proverbs 19:11; 1 Corinthians 9:24; Colossians 1:10, 11

ENERGY LEVEL: High
PLAYING TIME: 15 minutes

GOAL OF THE GAME: Avoid interferences to successfully cross the finish line.

Prior to playing, place the fabric squares end to end at one end of the playing area as the starting line. Place the jump rope at the opposite end of the playing area (at least 25 feet away). Set the rolling cube by the starting line. Have kids line up along the starting line.

LET'S PLAY!

Say: **Let's play a wild game called Interference. The word _interference_ means something that gets in the way, and in this unusual game, that's exactly what you'll be doing. I'll toss the rolling cube and call out the number, such as "four." When I say "Go!" everyone will run to the finish line, and the person who is the fourth one across the line becomes the Interferer and must try to get in the way of runners for the next race. The person who becomes the Interferer in the next race can help the first Interferer.**

Interferers can only stand to block the way of runners—tripping, grabbing, or holding out arms are not allowed. We'll keep rolling the cube and adding Interferers with each race until you'll have to zigzag like a rabbit to get across that finish line!

After each race, roll the cube again for a new number. The child who crosses the finish line in that place joins the other Interferers. Continue racing until two kids remain, then race until the first one crosses the finish line. Let the winner be the roller for the next game.

PLAYING PIECES

❏ Bible
❏ rolling cube (see page 6)
❏ 4 fabric squares
❏ jump rope

PLAYING TIPS

✔ *If your group is large, choose one child to toss the rolling cube and another child to count kids running across the finish line.*

45

Say: **Whew! That was some fast running even in the face of interference. You know, sometimes when we try to do good deeds or help others, things get in our way, too. Let's see what the Bible says about running the good race and how perseverance helps us finish the race.**

PEP TALK

Read aloud Proverbs 19:11; 1 Corinthians 9:24; and Colossians 1:10, 11. Then ask:

✔ *How is running a race like going through life?*

✔ *What things get in our way of following Jesus? of helping others?*

✔ *How can perseverance and patience help us finish the race?*

Say: **It can be hard running the race we call life. But we know the treasure that waits for us at the finish line—eternal life with Jesus! When things interfere or get in the way of us serving God or following Jesus, we have to keep going and get beyond the interference. Prayer, obeying God's Word, and trusting God to help us persevere are good ways to get past things that may interfere with the way we serve God or follow Jesus. Let's run our own good race again, except this time when you cross the finish line, shout "Perseverance helps!"**

RAINBOW CALL

Deuteronomy 10:20; Ephesians 6:7; Colossians 3:23

ENERGY LEVEL: Medium to high

PLAYING TIME: 15 minutes

GOAL OF THE GAME: Catch the tossed ball before your opponents do.

Prior to playing, make sure the day is not overly windy, since the beach ball might get carried away! Have kids "count off" according to the colors on the rolling cube— for example, red, green, yellow, blue, purple, and pink. (It's fine to have more than one of each color.) Instruct kids to stand in a large circle.

PLAYING PIECES

❏ Bible

❏ rolling cube
   (see page 6)

❏ beach ball

LET'S PLAY!

Say: **Nothing is quite so pretty as a rainbow, is it? And no game is quite so lively as Rainbow Call! In this game, I'll start off by standing in the center of the circle and rolling the cube. Then I'll toss the beach ball high in the air and call out the color that was rolled. Players with that color name are to rush forward to try and catch the ball before it touches the ground. Whoever catches the ball can be the next roller and tosser.**

After each catch, have kids form a large circle for the next toss. Continue until most or all players have had a turn to be the roller and tosser. Then say: **Rainbow Call is fun because you're on your toes until your color is called. That's how we should be when it comes to being called into service for God! Let's take a breather and learn why it's important to hop into action when God calls us to serve him.**

PEP TALK

Read aloud Deuteronomy 10:20a; Ephesians 6:7; and Colossians 3:23. Then ask:

✔ *In what different ways can we serve God?*
✔ *How is serving others a way to serve God?*
✔ *Why is it important to be ready to serve?*
✔ *What can we do to be ready to hop into action when God calls us to serve?*

Say: **God calls us to serve him in many ways. Sometimes it's through teaching or helping others, while at other times it's through praying for others or being encouraging with our words. Whatever the way, we want to be ready to serve God when he calls us. This time when we play Rainbow Call, let's call out each other's names. I'll toss the ball and call out someone's name. We'll see if that person is ready and can rush to catch the ball.**

POP TAG

Proverbs 7:2; 2 Thessalonians 3:3

ENERGY LEVEL: High
PLAYING TIME: 10 minutes

GOAL OF THE GAME: Be the last person with a balloon attached to your foot.

Prior to playing, be sure you have at least two balloons for each child. Have kids blow up and tie off one of their balloons. Tape the balloons to the kids' right shoes using a 2-foot piece of masking tape. Wrap one end of the tape around the balloons' knots and the other end around shoelaces or buckles.

PLAYING PIECES

❏ Bible
❏ masking tape
❏ package of balloons

LET'S PLAY!

Say: **You all have balloons following you, and it looks so colorful! We'll use the balloons to play a game called Pop Tag. In this fast-paced game, you'll try to pop other players' balloons by hopping on them while protecting yours from being popped at the same time. The object of the game is to be the last player with an unpopped balloon on your foot. It sounds easy, but watch out! It's not as easy as it looks. If your balloon is popped, you're tagged out and must sit in place and encourage others to watch out for hoppers 'n poppers!**

Have kids continue hopping and popping until only one player has an unpopped balloon on her foot. Then say: **That was fun but not as easy as it looked! Protecting what's valuable to us isn't always an easy job. Let's take a break and see how we can protect our treasures in Christ.**

PEP TALK

Invite volunteers to read aloud Proverbs 7:2 and 2 Thessalonians 3:3. Then ask:
✔ ***What treasures do we have in Jesus?*** (his love, forgiveness, eternal life)

✔ ***What sorts of things threaten to pop our treasures or steal them away?*** (lies, cheating, temptation to sin, hate)

✔ ***How can we protect what is ours in Christ Jesus?*** (through prayer, being obedient to God, trusting in God's protection, reading the Bible)

Say: **Lots of things in life try to pop or destroy the wonderful treasures we have in Jesus—but we want to protect those treasures. Through prayer, God's Word, being obedient to God, and following Jesus, we can help protect what is ours in Christ from being popped! Let's play Pop Tag once more, but this time hop to one end of the play area and back, being careful to protect your own and everyone else's balloons from popping. When you make it back to the starting place, shout "I can protect my treasures in Christ!"**

TAIL TAG

1 Corinthians 15:57; 2 Thessalonians 2:14; 2 Timothy 1:8, 9

ENERGY LEVEL: High
PLAYING TIME: 10 minutes

GOAL OF THE GAME: Join up with a tag team by snatching its tail.

Prior to playing, have kids form four tag teams and have one volunteer be It. Have tag teams stand in lines holding each other's waists so the first person is the head and the last player is the tail. Hand each player who is a tail a fabric square to tuck in his waistband or belt.

PLAYING PIECES

❑ Bible
❑ 4 fabric squares

LET'S PLAY!

Say: **What a wonderful day to chase and play! In this unusual game of tag, the object is for It to grab the tail of a tag team and shout**

49

"Bump!" The head of that tag team becomes the new It, and the player who snatched the tail tucks it into his waistband or belt and joins the team as the new tail. The new It must run to snatch the tail of another tag team and shout "Bump!" We'll continue until all the tails have new players.

When each tag team has a new tail, stop play and say: **You all worked hard to become part of a team! As Christians, we work hard being team members for Jesus, too. Let's cool down before another round and discover what it means to be part of Jesus' team.**

PEP TALK

Read aloud 1 Corinthians 15:57; 2 Timothy 1:8, 9; and 2 Thessalonians 2:14. Then ask:

✔ *What does it take to be a part of Jesus' team?* (kindness, love, serving others, asking his forgiveness)

✔ *How do we work as members of the same team to encourage others to join Jesus' team?*

✔ *Why do we want everyone to be a part of Jesus' team?*

Say: **Being a part of Jesus' team means many wonderful things. It means we treat others with kindness and love, we don't judge others, we pray and follow God's Word, and we work together to encourage others to join with Jesus. I like being part of Jesus' team, don't you? Let's form four new teams and play Tail Tag again. This time when you snatch a tail, shout "Join Jesus' team!"**

WATERWORKS

Ecclesiastes 4:12; Colossians 3:23; 1 Thessalonians 5:11

ENERGY LEVEL: High
PLAYING TIME: 15 minutes

GOAL OF THE GAME: Be the team to relay the most water across the playing field.

Prior to playing, fill a pitcher with water. Place four plastic tumblers side by side and about 5 feet apart. Place four more tumblers opposite the first set of tumblers and about 20 feet away. Have kids form four teams and stand at one end of the playing field, each team beside a tumbler. Fill the four tumblers with water and hand each child a plastic spoon.

LET'S PLAY!

Say: **What a great day for some cool water sports! In this relay race, called Waterworks, the object is to work with your team members to carry water from one tumbler to the one opposite yours using only plastic spoons. But in this relay, the team who wins is not the first to complete the task but the team who relays the most water into their cup. You'll have to carry carefully, carry quickly, and work together in this game!**

Have the first person in each line begin the relay by carrying a spoonful of water to the tumbler at the opposite end, then run back and pass the spoon to the next person in line. Continue until the first tumbler is empty.

When the all water has been relayed, compare the water levels in the cups and award the winning team an enthusiastic round of applause. Then say: **I think you all worked hard to get as much water as you did into the cups. Just look at what you've accomplished in the time you worked. Let's see what the Bible tells us about cooperation and working together for a common cause.**

PEP TALK

Read aloud Ecclesiastes 4:12; Colossians 3:23; and 1 Thessalonians 5:11. Then ask:
✔ *What is cooperation?*
✔ *How are cooperation and working together for a common goal related?*

✔ *Why do we need both to be successful in serving God?*

✔ *What are examples of how Christians work together for God?*

Say: **Cooperation and working for a common goal help keep us focused and on the same track. One person's energy, enthusiasm, and brains are great, but when we combine them with an entire team of people working together for God, just think how big that energy is! God wants us to combine our gifts and talents to serve him and help others. Cooperation takes a lot of patience, time, and kindness, but it works! So let's play Waterworks again, but this time let's work patiently and cooperatively to empty all the water back into the pitcher.**

PLAYING TIPS

✔ *Team this cool water game with the next one for some sunny summer fun!*

WATER CATAPULT

Psalms 23:5, 6; 68:35; Ecclesiastes 5:19; Philippians 4:19

ENERGY LEVEL: Medium to high
PLAYING TIME: 15 minutes

GOAL OF THE GAME: Be the team with the most water in your cup when time is called.

Prior to playing, fill two buckets with water. Have kids form from two to four teams, each with at least six players. Instruct each team to stand in two lines facing each other, as in the game diagram on page 53. Hand each player at the end of a lines a tumbler. Fill one of each team's tumblers with water.

PLAYING PIECES

❏ Bible
❏ 8 plastic tumblers
❏ 2 buckets of water

LET'S PLAY!

Say: **Are you ready for some wet 'n wild fun? In this game you'll be catapulting water back and forth down your line and back again. The object? Be the team with the most water in your** cup at the end of the relay. When I say "Go!" the players with water in their cups are to catapult the water to their teammates across from them, who will try to catch the incoming water in their cups. The tossers then quickly hand their cups to the

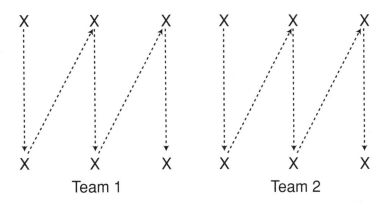

Team 1   Team 2

person beside them, who will try to catch the water tossed from the other players and so on. Continue passing cups and tossing and catching water until you reach the ends of your lines, then go back again.

When the relay is over, compare the amount of water in each tumbler, then have kids give each other high fives for a wet job well done. Then say: **What a cool, refreshing relay race that was. I noticed the water in your cups was almost overflowing at times. Did you know that the Bible speaks of a cup overflowing? Let's take a rest to dry off and discover what that cup is overflowing with!**

PEP TALK

Invite a volunteer to read aloud Psalms 23:5, 6; 68:35; Ecclesiastes 5:19; and Philippians 4:19. Then ask:

✔ *What do you suppose "my cup overflows" means?* (Lead kids to see that it means God's goodness to us is like a flood of love in our hearts and lives.)

✔ *What are good things God gives us in our lives?*

✔ *How can we thank God for his overflowing goodness?*

Say: **God's goodness and blessings are so great, they overflow and continue pouring out upon us from his abundant love. When we feel as if God's grace is overflowing in our lives, we want to pass that overflow on to others in the way of love, kindness, encouragement, and caring. That's pretty awesome, isn't it? Let's play our overflowing water game again, but this time we'll stand in a circle and play with two cups. We'll toss the water to opposite sides of the circle, and when you catch the water, tell one way God overflows your cup with blessings.**

SAUCER BOWLING

John 14:6, 10

ENERGY LEVEL: Medium
PLAYING TIME: 15 minutes

GOAL OF THE GAME: Be the team to knock over the last bowling pin.

Prior to playing, have kids form two bowling teams and stand facing each other, about 10 feet apart. Place the eight plastic tumblers in a line between the two teams and hand two players on each bowling team a plastic plate.

PLAYING PIECES

❑ Bible
❑ 8 plastic tumblers
❑ 4 plastic plates

LET'S PLAY!

Ask: How many of you have been bowling? Allow kids a moment to relate their bowling adventures, then say: **Let's play our own version of bowling, but instead of bowling balls, we'll toss flying saucers to knock over pins! When I say "Let's bowl!" the people holding the plates will sail the plastic-plate "saucers" toward the pins. If you knock one over, shout out "One!" and your team will have one point. If you knock over another pin, shout "Two!" and so on. The team to knock the last pin over is the winning team and can start the next game by tossing all four disks toward the pins. We'll play a couple of rounds of Saucer Bowling.**

After three or four rounds of Saucer Bowling, have the saucers land and say: **Bowling with flying saucers is a funny way to bowl, isn't it? You never know quite which path the saucers will take! I'm glad finding our way to God isn't so wiggly and wobbly and unpredictable. Let's take a break and learn where the straight, true path to God lies.**

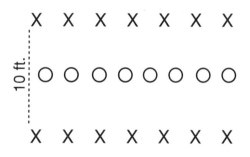

PEP TALK

Invite a volunteer to read aloud John 14:6, 10. Then ask:

✔ *Who is our pathway to God?*

✔ *In what ways does Jesus help lead us to God?*

✔ *How can staying on the right path to God help us every day?*

Say: **When we follow Jesus and obey his words, we're on the straight, true path to God. And we can know for sure that this path doesn't take any wobbly shortcuts or crazy changes in direction. When we love and follow Jesus, we stick to the straight path to God! Let's play another round of Saucer Bowling, but this time when you knock over a pin, instead of saying a number, shout "Jesus is the way to God!"**

BING, BANG, BONG!

Mark 16:15; John 13:34, 35; Galatians 6:10

ENERGY LEVEL: High

PLAYING TIME: 15 minutes

GOAL OF THE GAME: Be the first team to cooperatively catapult your items to the catchers.

Prior to playing, form two teams and have them stand at one end of the play area, about 6 feet apart. Place a fabric square, four tumblers, and two each of the following items beside each group: paint stir sticks, table-tennis balls, plastic plates, and crayons. Have each team choose four people to be their tossers, one to be the loader, and the rest to be catchers. Tell the catchers to stand 5 to 10 feet away from the tossers.

PLAYING PIECES

❏ Bible

❏ 2 fabric squares

❏ 8 tumblers

❏ 4 each of paint stir sticks, table-tennis balls, plastic plates, and crayons

LET'S PLAY!

Say: **Are you ready for a high-flying game full of fun and skill? Then let's play Bing, Bang,**

Bong! The object of this goofy game is to catapult items through the air to the catchers out in the field. The first team to successfully catapult all the items to its catchers is the winner. The tossers will hold the fabric square at the corners. Loaders will place an item from your pile on the fabric and say, "Bing!" Then the Tossers will catapult the item through the air and shout "Bang!" Finally, the catchers

will shout "Bong!" when they catch the items and place the items in a pile. If you miss a catch, run the item back to the loader and try again.

When the game is over, say: **Wow! That was a lot of high-flying fun, wasn't it? You were able to relay your items from one person to the next to the next in record time. When we tell others about Jesus, we relay an important message in much the same way. So let's take a breather and see how we can pass the Good News about Jesus from one person to another and relay the message around the world!**

PEP TALK

Read aloud Mark 16:15; John 13:34, 35; and Galatians 6:10. Then ask:

✔ *Why is it important to tell others about Jesus? to show Jesus' love through our actions?*

✔ *How can telling the Good News to one person spread the news to more people?*

✔ *In what ways does relaying the news about Jesus' love also relay hope and happiness to others?*

✔ *In what ways can you relay Jesus' love? the Good News about Jesus?*

Say: **When we make the effort to lovingly tell others about Jesus, the Good News just keeps spreading and spreading! And what's the best part?**

We are helping others when we share Jesus' love with them. Let's help our teams right now play another game of Bing, Bang, Bong! Change roles so the tossers are the catchers or loaders. And this time instead of shouting "Bing, bang, bong," let's shout "Spread Jesus' love!"

CAPTURE THE CUPS

1 Thessalonians 5:10; Hebrews 9:27, 28

ENERGY LEVEL: Medium
PLAYING TIME: 15 minutes

GOAL OF THE GAME: Help partners safely reach the base by blocking the tagger.

Prior to playing, have kids stand at one end of a large playing area. Place the jump rope opposite the kids and at least 20 feet away. Set the plastic tumblers behind the jump rope. Have kids form two teams: the runners and the taggers. Instruct the taggers to get with partners and to hook arms. Hand the fabric square "flags" to two players on the runners team and have them either hold the flags or tuck them in their waistbands. These players will run to capture the plastic tumblers.

PLAYING PIECES

- ❑ Bible
- ❑ 2 plastic tumblers
- ❑ stopwatch or timer
- ❑ jump rope
- ❑ 2 fabric squares

LET'S PLAY!

Say: **Let's play a fast-paced game called Capture the Cups. In this game, the two players with flags are the flag runners. The flag runners will try to capture the cups while avoiding the taggers, who must remain in pairs at all times. Now here's the twist in this tag-n-capture game: the runners' team can jump in the way and save their flag runners by being tagged themselves! In other words, runners can protect their flag runners by blocking taggers and taking the tag for their teammates. Each cup captured scores a point for the runners. You'll have five minutes to capture the cups, then we'll play again and switch team roles and flag runners.**

After kids have had turns being both runners and taggers, say: **Whew! That was a lot of fun and a lot of running. You did a great job of protecting your flag runners. And you unselfishly stepped in the way of the taggers to take the tags yourselves instead of letting the flag runners get tagged. You know, in much the same way, Jesus stepped in to protect us and took the punishment for our sins. Let's take a breather and see how Jesus blocked the way for our punishment and unselfishly took the sins of the world on himself.**

PEP TALK

Read aloud 1 Thessalonians 5:10 and Hebrews 9:27, 28. Then ask:

✔ *What did Jesus do to take away our sins?*

✔ *Why do you think Jesus unselfishly took away our sins instead of letting us be punished for them?*

✔ *How was Jesus' sacrifice a demonstration of his love for us?*

Say: **Just think of what Jesus did for us. He stood up for us and took the sins of the world upon himself so we wouldn't be punished with eternal death. Jesus died for our sins so we could have forgiveness and eternal life in heaven. Jesus loves us that much! Let's play Capture the Cups once more to remind us of how Jesus stood in the way of sin and eternal death for us with his perfect, unselfish love. This time when you capture a cup, give high fives and say, "Jesus' love has captured my heart!"**

GUARD BALL

Ecclesiastes 4:10-12

ENERGY LEVEL: High
PLAYING TIME: 15 minutes

GOAL OF THE GAME: Work with your partner to score points for your team.

Prior to playing, set up the playing area as for base-ball or kickball, with four plates as bases and the beanbag sock to mark the pitcher's mound (see below). Have kids form two teams and get with partners in their teams.

LET'S PLAY!

Say: **I have a new game for you today called Guard Ball. This game is played like baseball, but you and your partner must decide who will bat and run and who will guard from being tagged out. The runner will hit the pitched beach ball with her hands, then run to the first base. The guard will deflect anyone trying to tag the runner out. Guards cannot use their hands except to deflect the ball, but they can stand in the way of a tagger trying to tag out the runner. Each time a runner makes it back to home base, a point is scored for the team. When there are two outs, we'll switch, and the other team will be up to bat. The next time you and your partner get a chance to bat, switch roles so the runner becomes the guard. We'll play until one team scores five runs.**

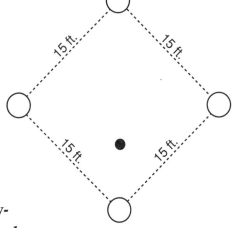

After one team has five points, have everyone sit down for a breather. Say: **You worked with your partners very well! It's fun to help our friends, and the Bible tells us that it's also an important thing to do. Let's take a seventh-inning stretch and see what the Bible teaches about helping our friends and family members.**

PEP TALK

Read aloud Ecclesiastes 4:10-12, then ask:

✔ *What are we to do for our friends and family members?*
✔ *Why is it important to be helpful and kind to friends and families?*
✔ *How does being kind to friends and family members strengthen our relationships with them? draw us all nearer to God?*

Say: **Because we care for our friends and the people in our families, we want to help them in times of trouble and to treat them kindly and respectfully all the time. Friends and families are lovely gifts from God, and we want to treat them that way. Now let's play another round of Guard Ball and form new partnerships with other friends as we play.**

LEAP THE LAKE

Exodus 14:19-22; 2 Corinthians 2:14; 2 Thessalonians 3:3

ENERGY LEVEL: High
PLAYING TIME: 10 minutes

GOAL OF THE GAME: See how far you can leap across the pretend lake.

Prior to playing, tape the paint stir sticks together, two and two. Place one set of sticks on a grassy area and lay the other sticks parallel and about 1 foot away from the first sticks to make the pretend lake. Have kids gather on one side of the lake and hand each player a paper plate.

PLAYING PIECES

❑ Bible
❑ masking tape
❑ paper plates
❑ 4 paint stir sticks

LET'S PLAY!

Say: **What a perfect day to go leaping and jumping like deer! How far do you think you can leap? Well, let's find out! This is our pretend lake** (point to the stir sticks)**, and we'll take turns leaping over it. After everyone has made a successful leap, we'll make the lake a bit wider and leap again. If you think that the lake is too wide, you may toss down your paper plate as a stepping-stone and leap from the stepping-stone to the other side. When you finally miss a leap even with the help of your stepping-stone, you can sit on the grass beside our pretend lake and cheer others on. We'll see how wide we can make the lake before no one can leap across it even with the help of a stepping-stone.**

Continue leaping and widening the lake. Move the sticks about 6 inches at a time. When most kids can't leap across even with the help of a stepping-stone, stop the game. Say: **That was some wide jumping, and it's a good thing you had the stepping-stones to help you! You know, Moses also had help crossing a sea once, but he didn't use a stepping-stone. Moses had much more powerful help! Let's take a break and see what special help Moses and the Israelites had when crossing the sea.**

PEP TALK

Invite volunteers to read aloud Exodus 14:19-22; 2 Corinthians 2:14; and 2 Thessalonians 3:3. Then ask:

✔ *What problems did Moses and God's people face?*

✔ *In what ways did God help Moses and the Israelites?*

✔ *In what ways might God help us step across troubles today?*

✔ *Why is it smart to rely on God's help in all situations?*

Say: **When we follow God's leading in our lives and rely on his help, we can find the way to overcome troubles. God is like a loving, heavenly stepping-stone helping us over problems we meet every day. I'm so happy that God is always ready to help us, aren't you? Now let's use our pretend stepping-stones to help us get over the make-believe lake. But each time you cross the lake, shout "God helps us!"**

CLEAN THE ATTIC

Deuteronomy 6:24, 25; 11:1; Luke 11:28

ENERGY LEVEL: Medium to high
PLAYING TIME: 10 minutes

GOAL OF THE GAME: Be the first team to relay your items from one end of the line to the other.

Prior to playing, choose at least eight pairs of items. Have kids form two lines and divide the pairs of playing items so each team has identical items. Instruct teams to place their items in a pile at the back of their team line. The playing items will be traveling from one end of each team's line to the other.

LET'S PLAY!

Ask kids if they've ever had a chore to do and if they got the job done quickly or put it off. Allow time for several responses, then say: **We have a lively job to do today! We're going to clean out our pretend attics by passing the items from the attic along the line to the make-believe dumpster at the other end of your line. But in this relay, you have to listen closely and follow directions carefully! I'll give several directions of how to pass each item. Each person in line must pass the item in the way I've instructed. When the items are almost through the line, I'll give new directions for passing the next item.**

Begin the relay by calling out an item, then giving passing instructions such as "Toss it up, clap, then pass it on." Use a series of fun passing directions for each item to keep the game moving and the kids listening. Other passing suggestions might include:

✔ *Tap the ground, turn around, then pass it on.*
✔ *Hop in the air, nod your head, then pass it on.*
✔ *Close your eyes, turn around, then pass it on.*

When both attics have been "cleaned," say: **Wow! You were good listeners and finished your cleaning job in record time. I think that's because you listened for directions and then promptly obeyed. Let's take a break and learn how important it is to listen to and obey God's directions.**

PEP TALK

Invite volunteers to read aloud Deuteronomy 6:24, 25; 11:1; and Luke 11:28. Then ask:

✔ *How does listening affect the way we obey?*
✔ *What things keep us from listening as we should? from obeying?*

✔ *Why is it important to listen to and obey God's directions and commands?*

✔ *In what ways can we listen to God more clearly? learn to be more obedient?*

Say: **Reading the Bible and praying are good ways to be sure we're listening to God. And when we carefully listen to what God tells us, we can obey more quickly. Let's play Clean the Attic again and see how quickly you can follow the directions I give you. Then we'll end with big high fives for our fellow cleaners.**

OVER THE RAINBOW

John 14:23; 15:7-11

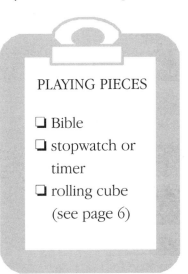

ENERGY LEVEL: Medium to high

PLAYING TIME: 15 minutes

GOAL OF THE GAME: Be the team with all but one player by the end of the game.

Prior to playing, "number" kids off by color, using red, yellow, blue, green, purple, and pink (the colors on the rolling cube). Form two teams and have kids stand in lines facing each other and about 15 feet apart. Have kids hold hands. This game is played like the classic Red Rover, but colors are called out instead of kids' names.

PLAYING PIECES

❏ Bible

❏ stopwatch or timer

❏ rolling cube (see page 6)

LET'S PLAY!

Say: **What a beautiful day for a rainbow! Let's play a game called Over the Rainbow and see how big of a rainbow we can make. In this game, one team tosses the rolling cube and calls out the color rolled. The players on the other team who have the color called run to gently break through the rainbow. Each person who breaks through may take a member of that team back to his own rainbow. But whoever doesn't break through must join that rainbow team and continue playing. We'll play for five minutes or until there's only one person left on a rainbow team.**

When there's only one player on a rainbow or five minutes have elapsed, call time. Then say: **What a fun game that was. You certainly switched back and forth between sides a lot! You know, that's one thing we never want to do when we follow Jesus. We want to stay on Jesus' side all the time, and that takes something called "commitment." Let's rest for a moment before playing another game and learn what being committed to Christ means.**

PEP TALK

Ask volunteers to read aloud John 14:23 and 15:7-11. Then ask:

✔ *What does it mean to be committed to Jesus?* (to trust him as our Savior, to give our lives to him, to stay loyal to him no matter what)

✔ *How does being committed to Christ change the way we think? the way we act?*

✔ *What can we do to stay committed to Jesus? to grow more committed?*

Say: **Commitment to Jesus means obeying and following him. It means not just following Jesus on Sundays, but every day. And it means putting Jesus first in our lives and always asking two powerful questions: "What would Jesus do?" and "What would Jesus say?" Being truly committed to Jesus is a lifelong attitude that comes from loving and following Jesus more closely every day. Let's play Over the Rainbow again, but this time, if you join a new rainbow, you cannot return to your old team. If you are chosen to return, say, "I'm committed to staying with Jesus!"**

Section 3:

QUICK-TIME PLAY

- ☑ rapid relays
- ☑ guessing games
- ☑ puzzles to ponder
- ☑ and more!

The sermon is running a little long, so grab a game and play along!

Here's a collection of quick games to fill those awkward moments when sermons are a bit too long, attention spans a tad too short, or time a bit too scarce. Every game in Quick-Time Play takes only about five minutes to play, and there's even a quick Bible message so you know you're offering fun with a focus even though time may be tight. From nimble number games and speedy spell-downs to rapid rounds of Human Tic-Tac-Toe and Hot-Potato Tennis, these games help you fill every moment with solid learning fun. Who says you need lots of time to play quality games? Now you're ready to offer games that are long on fun when time's a bit too short!

QUICK-TIME GAME TIPS

✔ Use quick games and lively activities to get the wiggles out and help kids refocus their energy on learning.

✔ When you're ready to play a quick game, clap your hands three times as a secret game signal and to grab kids' attention. When you finish playing, have kids clap three times as they return to their places and sit down to resume their regular classroom activities.

✔ Instead of a longer game, combine several quick games to keep kids interested, especially if your group is younger.

✔ Choose a boy to be Game King and a girl to be Game Queen for a day. Let each child choose a favorite quick-time game to play. Be sure to give every child a chance to be "game royalty" during the year!

NUMBER RUMBLE

John 10:3; Philippians 4:3; Revelation 3:5

ENERGY LEVEL: Medium
PLAYING TIME: 5 minutes

GOAL OF THE GAME: Run for the beanbag and switch places if your number is called.

Prior to playing, either set chairs in a large circle or have kids sit on the floor in a large circle (or on the outline of the indoor game floor, if it's set up). Number kids from one to six. There are many variations to this game, so try several to keep things interesting and kids on their toes!

PLAYING PIECES

❏ Bible
❏ beanbag sock
❏ rolling cube
(see page 6)

LET'S PLAY!

Say: **Let's play a quick game of Number Rumble. The object of this game is to snatch the center item and switch places in the circle as quickly as you can. I'll toss the rolling cube and call out a number. If your number is called, jump up and try to be the first to grab the beanbag, then find a place in the circle to sit before everyone else is seated. The player to grab the beanbag becomes the next tosser of the rolling cube.**

Play as time permits. For other variations, try one of the following:

✔ **Plus or Minus.** Older kids will enjoy the challenge of rushing for the beanbag when the number rolled can be added or subtracted to get their number. For example, a rolled 4 would allow the numbers 2, 3, and 1 to rush forward if you're playing addition (2+2, 3+1) or 6, 2, 5, and 1 if you're playing subtraction (6-2, 5-1).

✔ **Colors or Numbers.** Assign both numbers and colors so either a rolled color or number will get kids moving!

✔ **Twin Rollers.** Toss the rolling cube twice and call out both numbers at the same time.

After playing as many variations as time will allow, take a moment to say: **Just as we knew which numbers or colors we were in the game, God knows each of** our names, and they're written in his book of life. Let's take a moment to learn about God's special book.

PEP TALK

Read aloud John 10:3; Philippians 4:3; and Revelation 3:5, then ask:

✔ *How does God show his love for us by including us in his book of life?*

✔ *What do you think God's book of life reveals?*

✔ *How do knowing, loving, and following Jesus help us have a place in the book of life?*

Say: **The Bible tells us that God has a special book called the book of life. It's in this powerful book that God has written the names of his people—those who love and obey Jesus with all their hearts. Jesus calls us by name, and God knows our names as well. Those are special ways we know that we're loved by the Lord and called his own! Let's play another round of Number Rumble as you listen for your special number to be called.**

PROBLEM SOLVED!

Proverbs 2:6; Ecclesiastes 2:26; Daniel 2:20, 21

ENERGY LEVEL: Low
PLAYING TIME: 5 minutes

GOAL OF THE GAME: Work with a partner to solve a deceptively simple problem.

Prior to playing, have kids form pairs and hand each pair a paper plate. Invite pairs to find places around the room to stand.

LET'S PLAY!

Say: **Let's take a quick minute to see if you and your partner can figure out this little challenge. See if you can think of a way to stand together, side by side on your paper plate. What's the real**

PLAYING PIECES

❑ Bible
❑ stopwatch or timer
❑ 1 paper plate for every two kids

trick? Your feet cannot touch the floor in any way! In other words, you must figure out how you can both stand on the paper plate without touching the floor. I'll give you two minutes to try ways of standing on your plate, then we'll share the solutions you've discovered.

Allow kids to work on their problem solving for two minutes, then call time. Invite pairs to take turns demonstrating their solutions, which might include tearing the paper plate in half, standing on one foot, or even placing the center of the paper plate under a closed door and each partner standing on half of the plate.

After kids have shared their solutions, say: **You had some creative ways of solving this problem, which shows me that you used creativity, cooperation, and wisdom. Do you know where all your sound thinking and wisdom comes from? Let's take a short break to find out.**

PEP TALK

Invite volunteers to read aloud Proverbs 2:6; Ecclesiastes 2:26a; and Daniel 2:20, 21, then ask:

✔ *Where does true wisdom and understanding come from?*
✔ *Why does God want us to use our intelligence? our creativity?*
✔ *How can we put the wisdom that God gives us to use for him? to use for others?*
✔ *How can God help us grow even wiser?*

Say: **God gives us true wisdom and creativity because he loves us. God wants us to use our intelligence to solve life's problems, and he is always standing by to help, encourage, and show us the way. We can trust the wisdom that God gives us when we follow and obey him. In fact, obeying and loving God are the two smartest things we can do! Now let's see if you can figure out a way to both stand on the plate without touching each other at all!** If there's time, have kids also join with another pair, then challenge all four kids to stand on two plates without touching each other!

SURPRISE GIFTS

John 3:34; Romans 15:5; 1 Corinthians 15:57

ENERGY LEVEL: Low
PLAYING TIME: 5-7 minutes

GOAL OF THE GAME: Guess who presented you with a "special gift."

Prior to playing, place six crayons at the front of the room and have kids scatter and find places to sit around the room. If your group is ten or less, use only three crayons.

PLAYING PIECES

❏ Bible
❏ crayons

LET'S PLAY!

Say: **We only have time for a short game today, but this one isn't short on fun! In a moment, I'll choose several kids to come get these crayons while the rest of you hide your eyes in the crook of one arm and hold your other hand out. The crayon kids will tiptoe around the room and place their crayon "gifts" in waiting hands, then tiptoe to the front of the room again. We'll say, "Open your eyes and hold up your gift. Who has given you this wonderful gift?" Then you'll have a chance to guess who gave you the crayon. If you're right, you can give out the next gift. If your guess is wrong, the gift-giver goes again.**

Encourage kids to spread their gifts around so everyone has a turn to guess or give a gift. Then say: **This is a fun game, but the gifts are pretend. In real life, God gives each of us good gifts. Let's see what those gifts include.**

PEP TALK

Read aloud John 3:34; Romans 15:5; and 1 Corinthians 15:57. Then ask:
✔ *What wonderful gifts does God give to us?*
✔ *In what ways is Jesus God's greatest gift to us?*
✔ *How are God's gifts demonstrations of his love for us?*

✔ *Why is it important to use the gifts God gives us?*

Say: **God gives each of us good gifts to put to use serving him and helping others. God's gifts include blessings we can hold, such as good friends, loving family members, a nice house, and nutritious foods to eat. Gifts that we can feel include God's love, patience, wisdom, strength, and presence with us all the time. But the best gift of all is the victory God gives us through Jesus and his forgiveness! Let's play another round or two of Surprise Gifts. This time when you stand to guess who gave you the crayon, you must name a gift God gives to us.**

ON THE SPOT

Matthew 28:19, 20; 1 Thessalonians 2:8, 13; 1 John 1:3

ENERGY LEVEL: Low to medium
PLAYING TIME: 5 minutes

GOAL OF THE GAME: Tell something about Jesus if you land on the "spot."

Prior to playing, tape paper plates to the floor in a grid pattern, using five or more plates than the number of kids in your class. For example, for a class of fifteen kids, tape paper plates in five rows of four plates each. Use a crayon to color a large heart on one paper plate and a large cross on another. (Be sure the picture plates aren't side by side.) Have kids stand on the paper plates.

PLAYING PIECES

❏ Bible
❏ crayons
❏ paper plates
❏ masking tape

LET'S PLAY!

Say: **We have time for a quick game, so let's play On the Spot. I'll give a series of directions to help you travel along the giant paper-plate spots on the** floor, hopping from spot to spot. If you land on a spot with a picture, shout, "On the spot!" If you are on the plate with a heart, you must say something about Jesus' love, such as "Jesus' love is for everyone!" If you land on the cross, you must tell something about Jesus' help or what he has done for us, such as "Jesus died for our sins." Then we'll continue traveling with new directions. If you're at the end of a row and need to move more spots, simply hop to the nearest empty plate and continue moving.

Call out a series of hopping directions, such as, "Two spots right, one spot forward, two hops left." Younger children will probably do best with one or two directions at a time while older kids can handle a longer series. For variety, invite "guest callers" to give hopping directions. Stop between each set of directions to see if anyone is "on the spot" and wait for their responses.

After several sets of directions, say: **You moved quite a long way, and we heard some wonderful things told about Jesus. Let's take a moment to discover why it's important to tell about Jesus' love and forgiveness.**

PEP TALK

Read aloud Matthew 28:19, 20; 1 Thessalonians 2:8, 13; and 1 John 1:3. Ask:
- ✔ *How can telling others about Jesus' love and forgiveness help them? draw them closer to Jesus?*
- ✔ *In what ways does telling others about Jesus strengthen our faith? draw us nearer to Jesus?*
- ✔ *What could you tell someone about Jesus if they don't know him already?*

Say: **It only takes a moment to share Jesus with someone. Whether we remind a friend of how much Jesus loves her or tell someone about the power of Jesus' forgiveness, we're sharing Jesus and drawing others near to him. See if you can tell three things about Jesus to different people today. Now let's hop two times forward and tell one thing about Jesus to someone who lands near you!**

HUMAN TIC-TAC-TOE

Psalm 5:8; Matthew 7:13, 14; John 14:6

ENERGY LEVEL: Low
PLAYING TIME: 5 minutes

GOAL OF THE GAME: Work with your team to score a tic-tac-toe, three-in-a-row!

Prior to playing, stick a tic-tac-toe grid to the floor using masking tape. Make sure the squares are about 2 feet wide. Form two teams and assign one to be the Xs and the other team the Os. Have the Xs and Os stand on opposite sides of the game grid. Show the Xs how to hold their arms crossed in front of them as Xs, and have the Os form arm circles to show their team affiliation.

PLAYING PIECES

❑ Bible
❑ masking tape

LET'S PLAY!

Say: **We may not have lots of time, but there's always time for a quick game of Tic-Tac-Toe. And in this game, we'll use humans as the Xs and Os! Teams will take turns choosing where to place their team members on the grid. When a team has three players in a row, they can shout, "Perfect path!"**

Play a few games, encouraging teams to use different players to stand on the grid. Then say: **That was fun, wasn't it? You had to find straight paths to win the game, which is exactly what we do in our walk with Jesus! Let's take a quick break to learn what a perfect, straight path has to do with Jesus.**

PEP TALK

Invite volunteers to read aloud Psalm 5:8; Matthew 7:13, 14; and John 14:6. Then ask:

✔ *Who is our perfect path to God? What are other paths that don't lead to God?*

✔ *In what ways does staying on the path with Jesus help us find God? avoid troubles?*

✔ *How can we stay on the straight path to God?*

Say: **Obeying Jesus, being kind to others, praying, and reading God's Word are all good ways to stay on the straight path to God. And the best part? Jesus helps us stay on that path through his love, teaching, forgiveness, and guidance. We'll play our game once more, except this time when a team makes a straight, perfect path, let's all shout, "Jesus is the perfect path to God!"**

NIMBLE LIMBO

Psalm 46:1; Galatians 5:13; 1 Peter 4:10, 11

ENERGY LEVEL: Low to medium

PLAYING TIME: 5 minutes

GOAL OF THE GAME: Be the last player to make it successfully under the limbo sticks.

Prior to playing, tape the paint sticks end-to-end to make one long stick. Choose two volunteers to hold the ends of the limbo stick and direct kids to stand in two lines on opposite sides of the stick.

PLAYING PIECES

❏ Bible
❏ masking tape
❏ 4 paint stir sticks

LET'S PLAY!

Say: **Let's work out some of our wiggles and play a quick game of Nimble Limbo. In this game, two players will try to get under the limbo stick without touching the stick. Players can lean backward, crawl, or scooch under the stick. Players can also hold each other's arms or hands to steady one another. If any player touches the stick, he becomes a limbo stick holder and the holder joins that team. We'll play until no one can go under the limbo stick without touching it.**

Encourage pairs of kids to decide how they will go under the stick before they attempt the feat. As each pair slides successfully under the limbo stick, lead kids in a round of short applause. Continue until no pairs can get under the stick. Then say: **You really did a good job helping each other and leaning on one another.**

In fact, sometimes, the only way to get under the limbo stick was with your friend's help! Let's take a moment to see how leaning on God's help can see us through any problem.

PEP TALK

Read aloud Psalm 46:1; Galatians 5:13b; and 1 Peter 4:10, 11. Then ask:

✔ *Why do friends help one another and lean on each other?*
✔ *In what ways is God our closest friend and best helper?*
✔ *What kinds of troubles can God help us with every day?*
✔ *How does leaning on God and trusting in his help get us through tough times?*
✔ *How is God sending us good friends a powerful way to help us?*

Say: **Leaning on God means trusting him and having faith in the ways God can help. And those ways include God sending good friends our way or being sent to help someone else. It feels good to know that God is helping us all the time and that we can lean on his loving power to see us through the toughest of times. It also helps to know that we have friends God sends to lean on, too. Let's limbo once more, only this time after you and your partner go under the limbo stick, shout "Lean on God's loving help!" and give each other a big high five.**

GOAL ROLL

Psalm 105:4; Philippians 4:7; Hebrews 12:2

ENERGY LEVEL: Low to medium
PLAYING TIME: 5 minutes

GOAL OF THE GAME: Work with your team to capture the rolling ball.

Prior to playing, be sure the table-tennis balls are numbered with markers as 1 and 2. Have kids number off by twos and have both teams choose a player to be their team goalie. Have kids sit on the floor according to the game diagram and about 4 feet apart.

LET'S PLAY!

Say: **We have a few minutes to work off some wiggles, so let's play a cool game of Goal Roll. The object of this game is to roll your team ball, marked with either a 1 or a 2, to your team goalie—but it's not as easy as it looks! While you're trying to get your ball to your goalie, you must deflect the other team's ball from reaching their goalie. You may only roll the balls and use your hands to deflect the balls, and your bottom must stay seated at all times. When a goalie receives her team's ball, a point is scored. We'll play until one team wins two points. Remember, you'll need to keep your eyes on the goalie and both balls very carefully!**

Begin by rolling the numbered table-tennis balls to kids in line and begin the game. When a point is scored, stop the game and begin by rolling the balls over to start the next game. After one team has two points, say: **Wow! You really kept your eyes on the goal in this game, didn't you? Did you know we have a special goal in life to keep our eyes on? Let's take a moment to discover who we should keep our eyes on.**

	4 ft.	
team goalie 1	← - - - - →	2
2		1
1		2
2		1
1		2
2		1
1		2 team goalie

PEP TALK

Read aloud Psalm 105:4; Hebrews 12:2; and Philippians 4:7. Then ask:

✔ *As Christians, who are we to keep as our focus at all times?*

✔ *How can focusing on Jesus strengthen our faith? guard us? draw us closer to God?*

✔ *What might happen if we don't keep our eyes and hearts on following Jesus?*

Say: **It's so important to keep our focus on Jesus every day. Many things, such as lies, bad choices, and unkind thoughts, try to steer us away from following Jesus. But when we keep our hearts and minds focused on following Jesus and doing what he would do, we're all winners! Let's play Goal Roll one more time. When a point is scored, your team can shout, "Jesus is our goal!"**

GIGGLE-STOP

Psalms 32:11; 118:24; Romans 5:11; Philippians 4:4, 5

ENERGY LEVEL: Low
PLAYING TIME: 5 minutes

GOAL OF THE GAME: Be the first player to snatch the scarf from the dropper.

Prior to playing, choose one child to be the dropper and hand him the fabric-square "scarf." Tell the dropper to stand at one end of the playing area. Have the rest of the kids stand at the opposite end of the playing area.

PLAYING PIECES

❑ Bible
❑ 1 fabric square

LET'S PLAY!

Say: **Are you ready for a few good laughs? Then let's play a game of Giggle-Stop. In this game, the dropper will hold up the square scarf as you all walk heel-to-toe forward, laughing and giggling. But when the dropper drops the scarf, you must stop laughing and smiling and freeze in place. If you're caught with a giggle, you must return to the starting place and begin again. The first person to pick up the scarf becomes the next dropper.**

Be ready for loads of giggles, wiggles, and guffaws! When someone reaches the scarf, have kids sit in place and say: **What happy laughs and giggles I heard! You seemed to be having a good time playing—and a hard time keeping from laughing. You know, that's just how it should be when we feel the joy of Jesus! That joy should be so big in our lives that nothing can stop the good feeling. Let's take a moment to see why we have such unstoppable joy with Jesus.**

PEP TALK

Invite volunteers to read aloud Psalms 32:11; 118:24; Romans 5:11; and Philippians 4:4, 5. Then ask:

✔ **Why does knowing, loving, and following Jesus bring us great joy? help?**

✔ **How do we act when we have the joy of Jesus in our hearts and lives?**

✔ **What can we do to keep the joy of Jesus flowing in our lives?**

✔ **Why is it good to share this wonderful joy with others?**

Say: **When we have the joy of Jesus in our lives, it makes lots of changes in us. We want to help and be kind to others, learn more about Jesus, read the Bible, and pray to Jesus often. Having such deep joy in our hearts makes troubles easier to face, and even sadness isn't as sad. Let's play Giggle-Stop once again, but this time if you're caught smiling or laughing, say "I have the joy of Jesus in my heart" and keep playing from where you are.**

RAINBOW RACE

Genesis 9:14-16; 1 Kings 8:20; 2 Peter 3:9

ENERGY LEVEL: Medium
PLAYING TIME: 5-7 minutes

GOAL OF THE GAME: Find a base before you're tagged.

Prior to playing, stick a masking-tape line on the floor at one end of the playing area. This is the starting line. Use pink, red, purple, green, yellow, and blue crayons to make large hearts on the paper plates, one colored heart per plate. Tape the plates at the opposite end of the playing area and about 3 feet apart. (See illustration.) Have kids line up behind the starting line and assign them colors that match the rolling cube and plates. Choose one child to be the first Rainbow Roller and hand her the rolling cube. Position the Rainbow Roller in the center of the playing area and off to one side.

PLAYING PIECES

❑ Bible
❑ 6 paper plates
❑ masking tape
❑ 1 box of crayons
❑ rolling cube (see page 6)

78

LET'S PLAY!

Say: **Let's play a quick, lively game of Rainbow Race. The object of this game is not to get tagged as you're running to base. The paper plates at the opposite end of the room have colors that match the colors you've been given. The Rainbow Roller will roll the rolling cube and call out the color rolled. Players with that color will rush to stand on the paper plate that matches their color—**

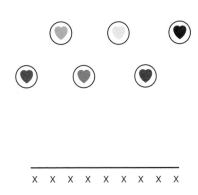

but without being tagged by the Rainbow Roller. You must have a foot or hand touching the base to be safe. If you're tagged, you'll become the next Rainbow Roller. We'll play until every color has been rolled at least one time.**

After every color has been rolled at least once, say: **That was lots of fun, wasn't it? Who can remember which Bible story tells us about the rainbow and what the rainbow means?** Allow time for kids to give their answers, then say: **Noah learned about God's promises through God's help and through the rainbow God placed in the sky. Let's take a moment to remember what God's promises mean to us today.**

PEP TALK

Read aloud Genesis 9:14-16; 1 Kings 8:20a; and 2 Peter 3:9. Then ask:

✔ *Why does God keep his promises?*
✔ *How is God's love shown through his kept promises?*
✔ *What are some of God's promises to us?*

Lead kids to recognize that God's promises include him always being with us, his love never ending, and his Word being true. Say: **God's promises are a sign of his love for us. And the rainbow is a sign that God keeps his promises just as he promised never to flood the world again. Let's play Rainbow Race once more, only this time we'll all run for bases and promise not to tag players with the color rolled!**

PLAYING TIPS

✔ *Try playing partner Rainbow Race and have partners run to their bases holding hands or with their elbows linked.*

BEACH BASKETBALL

Matthew 28:19; John 13:34, 35

ENERGY LEVEL: Medium
PLAYING TIME: 5 minutes

GOAL OF THE GAME: Shoot baskets as the beach ball travels around the room.

Prior to playing, have kids form groups of four and stand in mini circles around the room.

LET'S PLAY!

PLAYING PIECES

❏ Bible
❏ beach ball

Say: **We have a few minutes to get the wiggles out, so let's play a quick game of Beach Basketball. Choose someone in your group to be the first tosser and the rest of you stay in a circle and hold hands to make human basketball hoops. The tosser will toss the beach ball to the group standing next to her group and try to make a basket. Each time a basket is made, shout "One down, travel on!" Then that group's tosser will try for a basket with the group next to him. After you've been a tosser, join your group in making a hoop and choose a new tosser. We'll continue until everyone has been a tosser.**

When everyone has had a turn tossing the beach ball and trying to make a basket, sit in groups and say: **That was some fast-tossing fun! It was like we were traveling around the world making goals. Jesus wants us to have a similar goal in real life: going around the world to bring his love to others. Let's take a quick look at why we want others to know and follow Jesus.**

PEP TALK

Read aloud Matthew 28:19 and John 13:34, 35. Then ask:
✔ *How can knowing and following Jesus help us live?*
✔ *Why do we want others to know and love Jesus?*
✔ *In what ways does telling others about Jesus' love help them?*

Say: **Many Christians travel to other countries around the world to tell others about Jesus. These people are called "missionaries," and they live their entire lives serving Jesus and helping others. We can be missionaries right here at home by telling others about Jesus and his love. When we help someone know, love, and follow Jesus, they may tell others, who can tell even others, too. Pretty soon, the message about Jesus has traveled around the world! During the coming week, tell three people about Jesus and watch the love spread and grow!**

HOT-POTATO

James 4:7, 8; 1 Peter 5:8-10

ENERGY LEVEL: Medium
PLAYING TIME: 5-7 minutes

GOAL OF THE GAME: Don't get caught with the hot potato on your team's side when time is called.

Prior to playing, place a 6-foot masking-tape line across the center of the playing area. This is the pretend net. Form two teams and have each team spread out and kneel on opposite sides of the net. Divide the pairs of playing items, placing four of each on each side of the net. Hold the beanbag sock.

PLAYING PIECES

❏ Bible
❏ stopwatch or timer
❏ masking tape
❏ 1 beanbag
❏ 4 pairs of items (not using table-tennis balls)

LET'S PLAY!

Hold up the beanbag sock and say: **I have a pretend hot potato here, and we'll use it to play a fast game of Hot-Potato. In this game, each team starts out with ten points. You'll be quickly passing items back and forth over the net, and the hot potato will be in the mix. You must pass or toss the items low over the net, not throw them. We'll play for one minute, and the team with the most items on its side will lose one point. But** you especially don't want to get caught with the hot potato on your team's side of the net when time is called. If you do, you will lose two points. We'll play several rounds and see who has the most points at the end.

Begin the game by having kids toss the items back and forth, then slide the beanbag sock into play. Play at least three rounds and see which team has the most points. Then say: **That hot potato sure traveled back and forth quickly. You got rid of it like it was the chicken pox! And that's just the way God wants us to get rid of bad things in our lives. Let's take a quick break to see what things God wants us to avoid.**

PEP TALK

Read aloud James 4:7, 8a and 1 Peter 5:8-10. Then ask:
✔ *What are things that we as Christians want to avoid?*
✔ *How does God help us avoid evil? resist temptation?*
✔ *How does obeying, following, and loving God help us stay away from evil in our lives?*

Say: **We want to obey God and stay away from all evil and appearances of evil. The Bible tells us that where God is, there can be no evil. That's why always staying close to God is the best way there is to avoid bad things and evil troubles. In other words, when we stick close to God, we can toss evil away from us as quickly as a hot potato! Let's play one last round of Hot-Potato. This time, when I call "Stop!" the player holding the hot potato is to name one thing God wants us to stay away from, such as lies, cheating, or mean words.**

SPEED SPELL TAG

Matthew 9:37, 38; Ephesians 5:15, 16; 2 Thessalonians 2:14, 15

ENERGY LEVEL: Medium
PLAYING TIME: 5 minutes

GOAL OF THE GAME: Form groups without being tagged.

Prior to playing, clear a large playing area and have kids gather in the center. Hold the rolling cube.

LET'S PLAY!

Say: **This is a cool spelling game and a lively game of tag all rolled into one. In Speed Spell Tag, I'll roll the rolling cube and call out a number. As I spell a word with either three or four letters, you must run to form groups of the number rolled. When I finish spelling, I'll try to tag people not yet in groups. If I tag you, you can tell me what I spelled—if you're right, you can go free while I try to tag someone else. If everyone gets into groups before being tagged, I have to roll the cube again. But if I tag someone who doesn't know the word I spelled, he is the next roller. You'll have to listen carefully and move quickly to form your groups!**

Play several rounds of Speed Spell Tag. Use three-letter words for younger kids and four- or even five-letter words for older groups. After several rounds, say: **Wow! That was a fast game. Did you feel like time was running out as you ran to form your groups? That's called a "sense of urgency," and as Christians we have a sense of urgency in helping others come to know Jesus. Let's take a breather and learn why we're in a such hurry for others to know Jesus.**

PEP TALK

Invite volunteers to read aloud Matthew 9:37, 38; Ephesians 5:15, 16; and 2 Thessalonians 2:14, 15. Then ask:

✔ *Why do we want others to know, love, and follow Jesus?*
✔ *Why do we want to hurry in telling others about Jesus?*
✔ *What can we say or do to help others come to know Jesus?*

Say: **We want everyone to come to know Jesus, and there's not a minute to lose in telling them. The sooner people meet Jesus, the sooner they can feel his love and forgiveness and experience his loving help in their lives. There are so many people in the world that we need to feel a sense of urgency about sharing Jesus with them so they can fight evil and begin loving one another as Jesus does. Let's play Speed Spell Tag once more. This time we'll spell J-E-S-U-S. So if you're tagged, say "Jesus saves us" and continue playing.**

YOU CHOOSE!

Deuteronomy 30:15, 16; Joshua 24:15; 1 Corinthians 15:58

ENERGY LEVEL: Medium
PLAYING TIME: 5 minutes

GOAL OF THE GAME: Help your team finish the relay race in creative ways.

Prior to playing, clear a playing area and place a 5-foot-long masking-tape starting line across one end of the playing area. Have each child choose a playing item. Form three or four teams with equal members and have them stand in relay lines behind the starting line. Place the plastic plate at the opposite end of the playing area. (If one team has an extra player, have him partner with a team member.)

PLAYING PIECES

❏ Bible
❏ 1 plastic plate
❏ masking tape
❏ one playing item from the Game Kit for each child

LET'S PLAY!

Say: **We have a few minutes for a lively relay race. The object of the relay is to travel to the plastic plate, touch it with your foot, then return to your team and sit down while another player has a turn. But how will you travel to the plate? You choose! You can choose to hop, skip, crawl, or twirl your way to the plate, but you must hold your playing item on your head at all times! If your item drops, pick it up and replace it on your head before continuing. We'll play until every team is seated.**

When everyone has had a turn traveling to the plate and kids are seated with their teams, ask kids why they chose to travel in the ways they did. After several responses, say: **There were some fun choices, some challenging choices, and even some clever choices made in this game. Some choices were made for speed, and some just for silliness. The choice was**

		starting line
X	X	X
X	X	X
X	X	X
X	X	X
Team 1	Team 2	Team 3

yours! Let's take a moment to see how God gives us a very important choice to make every day.

PEP TALK

Read aloud Deuteronomy 30:15, 16; Joshua 24:15; and 1 Corinthians 15:58. Then ask:

✔ *Why does God want us to choose who we will serve?*

✔ *Why doesn't God force us to serve him?*

✔ *In what ways is this a choice we must make every day of our lives?*

✔ *How does our choice to serve God show our love for him? our faith in him?*

Say: **God wants us to freely choose to love and serve him. He also wants us to make that choice every day—it's that important! When we freely choose to serve God, it shows our love for him and our choice and desire to obey and follow God in all we do. Let's form new teams and play our relay again. This time as you touch the plate with your foot, say "I choose God today and always!"**

LOONY BALLOON

Psalm 85:8; Acts 10:33; James 1:22

ENERGY LEVEL: Medium

PLAYING TIME: 5 minutes

GOAL OF THE GAME: Be the first player to reach the caller.

Prior to playing, hand each child a balloon to inflate and tie off. The teacher can be the caller or choose a child to call out directions. Have kids stand at one end of the playing area and position the caller at the opposite end.

LET'S PLAY!

Say: **Are you good and careful listeners? Well, let's find out in this funny game called Loony**

PLAYING PIECES

❑ Bible

❑ balloon for each player

85

Balloon. This game is played much the same as Mother, May I? The object is to be the first player to tap my shoe. I'll give various directions, such as "Balloons between your knees, then hop forward two hops." Listen carefully, then follow the directions. If someone misses a direction, he must return to the starting line.

Begin the game and use the following directions before making up more of your own.

✔ *Balloons on your heads, then tiptoe three steps.*

✔ *Balloons under your chins, then hop on one foot one time.*

✔ *Balloons between your ankles, then two steps backward.*

✔ *Balloons on your tummies, then crab-walk four steps.*

When a player taps your shoe, have everyone sit in place. Say: **That was loads of fun, but it took lots of listening to get the directions straight. Why do you think listening to God is so important? Let's find out!**

PEP TALK

Invite several volunteers to read aloud Psalm 85:8; Acts 10:33b; and James 1:22. Then ask:

✔ *How can listening carefully to God help us obey God? steer clear of evil?*

✔ *What might happen if we ignore God and his rules?*

✔ *How can reading the Bible, learning God's Word, and going to church help us listen better to God?*

✔ *Why is just listening to God not enough? Why is it important to obey God after we listen to him?*

Say: **We listen to God through prayers, through reading the Bible, and through the feelings he gives us in our hearts. And when we know what God is saying to us, we can obey him better. Listening to God shows that we care about what he has to say and demonstrates our trust and love for him.**

If there's time, play another round of Loony Balloon. If you prefer, try one of the versions in the tips box.

PLAYING TIPS

✔ *Use balloons to play Simon Says or even a quick game of balloon volleyball, using a line of chairs for a net.*

GO GRASSHOPPER!

John 14:2, 3; 2 Peter 3:13

ENERGY LEVEL: Medium to high
PLAYING TIME: 5 minutes

GOAL OF THE GAME: Hop to your "homes" with your partner grasshoppers.

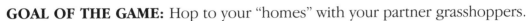

Prior to playing, lay the jump rope at one end of the playing area as the starting line. Set the paper plates at the opposite end of the play area. Be sure there is at least 10 feet between the starting line and the paper plates, and make sure you have one plate for every 2 or 3 players. Instruct kids to find partners and assign partners one of the colors on the rolling cube. Position partners behind the starting line and opposite their paper plates. Hold the rolling cube.

PLAYING PIECES

❑ Bible
❑ 1 jump rope
❑ 1 paper plate for every 2 to 3 players
❑ rolling cube (see page 6)

LET'S PLAY!

Say: **Let's all turn into pretend grasshoppers for this game that's just hopping with fun! In Go Grasshopper! you and your partner will hop toward your paper-plate house. I'll roll the rolling cube twice, once to call out the number and once to call out a color. Grasshoppers with the correct color will hop the number of hops called. For example, if I roll a number two and red, only red grasshoppers will take two hops toward their homes. Partners must stay close beside each other as they hop along. When you reach home, sit on the paper plates. We'll play until all the grasshoppers have reached their homes.**

When all of the grasshoppers are sitting on the paper plates, say: **You looked like happy grasshoppers on your way home. You know, we all have homes we live in, too—but did you know that Jesus is preparing us another home? Let's rest for a moment as we discover what our home in heaven will be like.**

PEP TALK

Read aloud John 14:2, 3 and 2 Peter 3:13. Then ask:

✔ *Why do you think Jesus is preparing us a place in heaven?*

✔ *How does knowing we'll live with Jesus in heaven someday affect how we feel and act today?*

Say: **Jesus loves us and wants all of us to live with him in heaven someday. It makes me feel good to know that Jesus is making a place for us. And, oh, how beautiful that home will be! Let's play our hopping game again, except this time when you reach home, shout "Heaven is our best home!"**

If there's time, play this game once more, but have boys hop on the odd numbers rolled and girls hop on the even numbers.

BULL'S-EYE

Matthew 18:3, 4; John 14:2, 3; Galatians 3:29

ENERGY LEVEL: Medium
PLAYING TIME: 5-7 minutes

GOAL OF THE GAME: When you get the signal, rush around the circle and find a place to sit before you're tagged.

Prior to playing, inflate and tie off two balloons. Have kids sit in a large circle on the floor. Be sure there's several feet behind the circle for running room. Choose one player to stand in the center. Hand two players on opposite sides of the circle each a balloon.

PLAYING PIECES

❏ Bible
❏ 2 balloons

LET'S PLAY!

Say: **Let's use these few minutes to get the wiggles out and have a bit of fun playing a game called Bull's-Eye. In this game, the player in the center will think of a letter of the alphabet and whisper that letter to me. Then we'll begin passing the balloons and repeating the alphabet. When we say the chosen letter, the player in the center will shout "Bull's-eye!" Then the two players holding the balloons must hop up and skip or hop around the circle to the right, trying to find a place to sit. The player in the center can rush to sit in one of the empty places. Whoever is left without a place to sit becomes the next player in the center.**

After several rounds of Bull's-Eye, say: **Whew! It feels odd to be left without a place to sit, doesn't it? It's a good thing we all have a place in God's kingdom! Let's take a break and discover what it means to have a place in God's kingdom.**

PEP TALK

Invite volunteers to read aloud Matthew 18:3, 4; John 14:2, 3; and Galatians 3:29. Then ask:

✔ *In what ways do we have a place in God's heart and his kingdom? in our church family?*

✔ *How does belonging to Jesus and loving him help us know we have a place in God's kingdom?*

✔ *How does knowing you have a special place in God's heart as well as right here in our church make you feel?*

✔ *How does being a member of God's family help us be kind to others? help them? share God's love with others?*

Say: **When we love and obey God, we don't have to worry about not having a place in his heart or in his kingdom. So if you ever feel left out or like you don't belong, just remember that you have a special place both here on earth as well as in heaven!** Play Bull's-Eye once more if there's time, but this time have kids offer a spot for someone to sit as they run around the circle.

DEFLECT-N-PROTECT

Psalms 91:1-4, 11, 12; 116:6

ENERGY LEVEL: Medium
PLAYING TIME: 5-7 minutes

GOAL OF THE GAME: Be the team with the most points left after five minutes.

Prior to playing, be sure the indoor game floor is in place. Blow up and tie off eight balloons. Have kids form four teams and each sit in a triangular portion of the game floor.

LET'S PLAY!

Say: **Let's fill these extra minutes with a lively game of Deflect-n-Protect. This game is played a bit like volleyball, except we'll use several balloons instead of a ball. Each team will start with five points, and the object is to protect your points as you deflect the balloons from landing in your area. We'll volley the balloons back and forth between teams, but if a balloon lands on a team's portion of the game floor, that team has one point subtracted from its score. You can only bop and deflect the balloons with your hands, and your bottoms must stay on the floor at all times. At the end of five minutes, we'll see which team has the most points remaining.**

Begin the game by tossing all eight balloons in the air above the game floor. After five minutes, call time and say: **What a cool game! And you all worked so hard protecting your points. Did you know that God works hard all the time to protect us, too? Let's take a break and discover why God protects us so carefully and continually.**

PEP TALK

Invite volunteers to read aloud Psalms 116:6 and 91:1-4, 11, 12. Then ask:
✔ *Why do you think God wants to protect us?*

> ### PLAYING PIECES
>
> ❑ Bible
> ❑ stopwatch or timer
> ❑ 8 balloons
> ❑ indoor game floor (see page 8)

✔ *How does God's protective care show his love?*

✔ *In what ways does God protect us?*

Say: **Just knowing that God is with me and watching out for me is such a good feeling. It helps me trust God even more. God protects us in so many ways, too. He provides his Word for us to read, learn, and use. He sends angels to cover us and guide us away from harm. Best of all, God sent Jesus and the Holy Spirit to be our protectors and guides. Just think how God loves and values us to give us such constant loving protection! Let's play Deflect-n-Protect once more to remind us how God deflects troubles from us and covers us with his protective love.**

PLAYING TIPS

✔ *Play another version of Deflect-n-Protect by having groups of four try to protect plastic tumblers from being knocked over by other groups rolling the beach ball.*

Section 4:

QUIET-TIME GAMES

☑ memory matches

☑ problem solvers

☑ terrific travel games

☑ and more!

Quiet and calm—are kids ever this way? But that's just the game you need to play!

We all know that kids love rowdy, rambunctious games, but that's not always possible. Your mission? Show kids that they can have tons of fun playing quiet games. This collection of low-energy entertainment includes games appropriate for cooldown times, small classroom fun, trips and travel—even quiet learning enrichment. Memorable memory matches, perfect puzzlers, great guessing games, and more highlight Quiet-Time Games and offer calm learning fun for those moments when you need to capture kids' energy but not squelch their spirits!

QUIET-TIME GAME TIPS

✔ Signal the beginning of quiet time by flipping the lights a few times, then leaving them off (unless the room goes pitch black!) for a few moments. Give kids directions, then turn the lights back on.

✔ Speak in a lower-than-normal voice so kids have to be very quiet to hear directions.

✔ Encourage partner play to keep kids in one place and more calm.

✔ Take *Collect-n-Play Games for Kids* along on class trips, picnics, retreats, or other times you may need a quiet game to pass the time.

I REMEMBER...

Psalm 103:12; Luke 7:47, 48; 1 John 2:12

ENERGY LEVEL: Low

PLAYING TIME: 15 minutes

GOAL OF THE GAME: To recall and repeat an entire list of playing items.

Prior to playing, invite kids each to choose a playing item. Then have kids sit in a circle and keep their playing items hidden in their laps.

PLAYING PIECES

❑ Bible
❑ a playing item for each child

LET'S PLAY!

Say: **Let's see how good your memories are today. We'll play a game called I Remember... The game begins with someone saying, "I remember September when I bought a..." and holding up her playing item and saying its name. Then the next person will say, "I remember September when I bought a...," and he will name the first item and then add his own item to the list. As each item is named in the list, hold the item up, then hide it again. If you have trouble remembering an item, you can call on someone to help. We'll continue listing items until one of you can repeat the entire list!**

After playing, say: **Wow! You need to have a good memory to remember all the items. Most of the time having an accurate memory is good, but there's one time when God chooses not to remember. Let's take a break to discover when God chooses not to remember.**

PEP TALK

Read aloud Psalm 103:12; Luke 7:47, 48; and 1 John 2:12. Then ask:

✔ *What do you think it means that God chooses not to remember our sins?*

✔ *Why do you think God chooses not to remember our sins?*

✔ *Why is it important to change our behavior after being forgiven?*

✔ *How does knowing that God does not remember our sins or keep score help us?*

Say: **God loves us and knows there are times when we slip up. After all, the Bible tells us in Romans 3:23 that we've all sinned and fallen short of God's glory. That's why it's wonderful that God chooses not to remember our sins once we have been forgiven. We can begin new and fresh and do things right! I'm so glad that God doesn't hold grudges and gives me a new chance to be the kind of person he desires me to be, aren't you? Let's trade items and play I Remember... once more, except this time, if you can't remember an item, we will all say, "God remembers our sins no more!" and take that item off our list!** Place the removed items in the center of the circle.

PLAYING TIPS

✔ *For a variation, form two teams and have one team hold up its items for fifteen seconds, then hide them. See how many items the other team can remember.*

BETTER LETTERS

2 Corinthians 9:10-15; Ephesians 1:3

ENERGY LEVEL: Low
PLAYING TIME: 15 minutes

GOAL OF THE GAME: Earn points by adding your team's letters to make longer words.

Prior to playing, hand each player an index card. Have kids form five teams and give each team two or three crayons. Tell kids to decide with their teams what letters they want to write on their cards, one letter per card. Have each team be sure to include at least one vowel.

LET'S PLAY!

Say: **Here's a game that's as fun to play as it is to think about. The object of Better Letters is to keep adding letters to make new words until no more**

PLAYING PIECES

❏ Bible
❏ 1 index card for each player
❏ crayons

96

letters can be added. **Each time a team adds a letter to make a new word, they'll score a point. If no more words can be made and your team added the last letter, you'll receive five bonus points. We'll begin by having one team come to the front of the room and hold up a letter, for example the letter "O." If another team has a letter that can be added to make a new word, such as the letter "T" to make the word "to," they can jump up and add the letter and read the new word. Then that team will score one point. If some team can add another letter to make a new word, such as "E" to make "toe," they'll score a point. We'll play five rounds so each team has a chance to start the game. Keep track of your own scores.**

Begin play by choosing a team to hold up a letter. Once letters are in place, they cannot be rearranged—teams may add letters to the beginning or end of the word. Teams may add as many letters as possible during each round of play. When no more words can be made, award five points to the team adding the final letter and begin a new game.

After five rounds, say: **That game was exciting as more and more letters were added together. God's blessings are exciting when they're multiplied, too. God adds blessings into our lives the more we know and love him! Let's take a quick break to see how God adds blessings into our lives.**

PEP TALK

Invite volunteers to read aloud 2 Corinthians 9:10-15 and Ephesians 1:3. Then ask:
✔ *What kinds of blessings does God give us?*
✔ *What does God want us to do with the good things he gives us?*
✔ *Why do you think God wants to give us more blessings and good things?*
✔ *How can we thank God for multiplying his blessings to us? How can we share our blessings with others?*

Say: **God gives us good things because he loves us. God also gives us good things when we obey him by following his commands. God's blessings are a demonstration of his great love for us, and they just seem to grow and grow. And you know the best part? When we share God's blessings with others as he desires us to do, he multiplies them even more! Let's see if we can use our letter cards to make words that name God's blessings, such as the words** *love, peace, truth, joy,* **and** *Jesus.* Make as many words as possible with your cards. Consider making letter cards to fill in missing letters you may need. Then tape the cards to the wall as a reminder of your fun game and God's good blessings!

SPELLING BEE

Deuteronomy 32:3, 4; Hebrews 13:15

ENERGY LEVEL: Low
PLAYING TIME: 15 minutes

GOAL OF THE GAME: Help your team guess the opponent's word by spelling it with a jump rope!

Prior to playing, have kids form two teams. Hand each team five index cards and a crayon. Challenge teams to write words that praise God on the cards. Suggestions for praise words might include "almighty," "divine," "powerful," "Father," "loving," and "forgiving." Tell teams that longer words will be more challenging to guess—but they need to make sure that the words are spelled correctly! When the cards are complete, have each team place its cards face down in front of them.

PLAYING PIECES

❑ Bible
❑ 10 index cards
❑ 2 crayons
❑ stopwatch or timer
❑ jump rope

LET'S PLAY!

Say: **Who's ready for an old-fashioned spelling bee? Our spelling game has a modern twist, though! One team will choose a pair of players to select a word card from the other team, then those two players will use the jump rope to spell out the letters to that word as their teammates try to guess the word in three minutes or less. If a team guesses the word, they must shout it aloud. If they're correct, the opponents will give a thumbs-up signal, and the spelling team will score one point. If the word is incorrect, the opponents will give a thumbs down, and the spellers must continue until time runs out.**

Play until all the word cards have been spelled, then award the team with the highest score pats on the back. Say: **There are lots of good spellers in this room! And there were also lots of powerful praise words used in our game. The praise words you wrote and spelled all honor God and tell about who he is. Let's take a break to discover why praising God and speaking words of praise are powerful ways to tell God how much we love and want to honor him.**

PEP TALK

Invite volunteers to read aloud Deuteronomy 32:3, 4 and Hebrews 13:15. Then ask:

- ✔ **In what ways do our words show our feelings?**
- ✔ **How do words of praise tell God how we feel about him?**
- ✔ **Why do we want to praise God every day and give him honor and glory?**

Say: **Praising God is a good way of expressing how we feel about God and of telling God we love him. We can praise God in our prayers, in songs, in poems, and in the way we tell others about him. So let's honor God right now by taking turns reading our praise words aloud. Then we'll end with a big "amen."** If there is time, tape the praise cards to ribbon, string, or yarn and suspend the words from a ceiling or doorway.

PLAYING TIPS

✔ *Play this active game using Bible characters' names, books of the Bible, or places in the Bible. What a great way to enrich the learning and increase the fun!*

PUZZLE POP

Psalm 119:1, 2, 7, 8, 11, 104, 105

ENERGY LEVEL: Medium
PLAYING TIME: 15 minutes

GOAL OF THE GAME: Be the first team to reassemble the Scripture verse.

Prior to playing, form four teams. Hand each person a balloon and each team a crayon and an index card. (Make sure each team has the same number of balloons.) Have each team choose one of its players to be the scribe and write Psalm 119:11 on an index card with a crayon. (If your kids are older, use verses 11 and 12.) Tell teams to carefully tear the index cards into as many pieces as they have balloons. Then have each player gently insert a piece of the puzzle into a

PLAYING PIECES

- ❏ Bible
- ❏ balloons
- ❏ index cards
- ❏ crayons

balloon, blow it up, and tie it off. Direct teams to exchange balloons and stand at one end of the playing area. (Hint: You may wish to use several different verses of approximately the same length. Write the verses on paper for kids to copy onto their index cards.)

LET'S PLAY!

Say: **This is a zany relay race to help us learn a little bit of God's Word. In this Scripture relay, each person will bop a balloon to the other end of the playing area, then sit on the balloon to pop it and retrieve the puzzle piece inside. When all the pieces are collected, work with your team to reassemble the verse. As soon as you have the complete verse put together, put your hands on your hearts.**

When the verses are complete, have teams read them. Award the winning team a lively round of high fives. Then say: **There are lots of ways to learn God's Word. Let's take a break and discover why it's important to learn God's Word and check out some good ways to learn Scripture.**

PEP TALK

Have volunteers read aloud Psalm 119:1, 2, 7, 8, 11, 104, 105. Then ask:

✔ *Why do you think learning God's Word is so important?*

✔ *What does it mean to use God's Word as a lamp to our feet and a light for our paths?*

✔ *How can God's Word help us avoid troubles? strengthen our faith?*

Say: **God wants us to learn his Word because it teaches us how to love and obey God and how to be kind and forgiving to others. In other words, God's Word helps us live the way God wants us to live. Now that's important! We can learn God's Word through singing Scripture songs, through reading the Bible, through word games, and even through Scripture puzzles and relays. So let's have another special relay to help us learn God's Word.**

We'll place the Scripture puzzle pieces in two piles at the end of the room. Then we'll take turns bopping a balloon back and forth as two players from each team walk to the piles, choose puzzle pieces, then return to their teams so two more players can go. When you have all your pieces, put the verse together and shout, "God's Word helps us win!"

OH, THAT HAT!

Genesis 16:13; Psalms 33:13-15; 139:1-4

ENERGY LEVEL: Low
PLAYING TIME: 10-15 minutes

GOAL OF THE GAME: Guess which hat your opponent's cotton ball is hiding under.

Prior to playing, have kids form two teams and hand each team four plastic tumblers and a cotton ball. If you class is small, you may use as few as two tumblers per team. Tell teams to sit in lines facing each other and about 10 feet apart. Young children especially love this hide-n-seek game!

PLAYING PIECES

❏ Bible
❏ 8 plastic tumblers
❏ 2 cotton balls

LET'S PLAY!

Say: **Let's turn our attention to a different kind of hide-n-seek game. In this game, teams take turns guessing under which plastic-cup "hat" the other team's cotton ball is hiding. When I say, "Hide inside!" teams will turn their backs on one another and quickly choose someone to slide the cotton ball under her hat. Three hats on each team will have nothing under them, and one will have the hidden cotton ball. When I say, "Turn around—let's see what's found," teams will turn around, holding onto their hats, and we'll take turns guessing which hats the cotton balls are hiding under. If a team guesses on the first guess, they score three points. You'll score two points for two guesses, and one point if it takes three guesses. Teams will keep track of their own scores, and we'll play to ten points.**

When one team reaches ten points, say: **It's not always easy to guess where something or someone is hidden. That's because we don't have superpowers to see through things and to know everything. Think about the time Jonah tried to hide from God before being swallowed by a big fish. Who saw Jonah and knew right where he was all the time?** Allow kids to tell that God knew and saw Jonah. Continue: **Let's take a moment to discover how God sees us all the time.**

PEP TALK

Invite volunteers to read aloud Genesis 16:13 and Psalms 33:13-15; 139:1-4. Then ask:

✔ *How does it feel to know that God sees us and cares about where we are?*

✔ *Can we hide our thoughts and feelings from God? Why or why not?*

✔ *How can knowing we can't hide from God keep us honest? help us be strong and courageous? fill us with faith?*

Say: **Jonah couldn't hide from God, and neither can we. God sees and knows all we do all the time. We can't hide from God, but we can find shelter in God's love and protection. I'm glad God sees me and knows where I am and what I'm thinking, because that shows he loves me a whole lot! Let's play our hide-n-seek hat game again. This time when the hidden ball is found, shout "God sees us all the time!"**

MATCHMAKER

Matthew 7:21; James 2:14; 1 John 3:18

ENERGY LEVEL: Low
PLAYING TIME: 15 minutes

GOAL OF THE GAME: Make the most match-ups with the least guesses for your team.

Prior to playing, choose pairs of Game Kit items that can be easily hidden in laps, such as table-tennis balls, cotton balls, crayons, plastic spoons, and uninflated balloons. You'll need a set of items for every two players. Place the playing items off to one side of the playing area. Have kids form two teams and designate one team the Hiders and the other the Matchmakers. Instruct the Matchmakers to choose one person to be the scorekeeper and hand that player a crayon and an index card.

LET'S PLAY!

Remember the old television game show called *Concentration?* This cool game is played in much the same way! Say: **Let's play a game in which we match up pairs of items. In a moment, the Matchmakers will turn around so they can't see the Hiders choose pairs of playing items. The Hiders will form partners, and each set of partners will choose a pair of playing items, then find a place to sit at the front of the room. Partners can sit together or fool the other team by sitting away from their matching item. The Hiders will hide the playing items in their laps. Then the Matchmakers will take turns calling out the names of two Hiders. Those Hiders will reveal their items. If it's a match, the Hiders with the items will sit off to the side. If it's not a match, the Hiders will hide their items in their laps and wait to be called again. The scorekeeper is to keep track of all the guesses. We'll see how many guesses it takes the Matchmakers to match up all the items. Then we'll switch game roles and play again.**

When kids have been both Hiders and Matchmakers, say: **That was a good game, and it really stretched our match-up abilities. As Christians, we want to make good match-ups between what we say and what we do. Let's take a break and see how important it is for our words and actions to match.**

PLAYING TIPS

✔ *If you have an extra child on a team, have him be the scorekeeper or use three of one item and call this the bonus match.*

PEP TALK

Invite volunteers to read aloud Matthew 7:21; James 2:14; and 1 John 3:18. Then ask:

✔ ***What kinds of things do we say or speak of when we love Jesus?*** (the truth, kind words, encouragement, and prayers)

✔ ***What kinds of things do we do as Christians?*** (serve God, help others, act kind and loving to parents)

✔ ***Why is it important that the way we speak and act match up?***

Say: **If we speak kindly to someone but then treat that person rudely, that's not a good match and would hurt the person's feelings. But when we speak with loving-kindness and truth and then back it up with kind and honest actions, we have a perfect match! And that's just what Jesus wants us to have! Jesus' words and actions matched, and we want ours to do the same. Let's play Matchmaker again and this time if you make a match, shout "I want to match Jesus in word and in deed!"**

TALL TOWERS

Proverbs 8:13; 11:2; 16:5, 18

ENERGY LEVEL: Low
PLAYING TIME: 10-15 minutes

GOAL OF THE GAME: Build the tallest tower in three minutes without tipping it over.

Prior to playing, choose items from the Game Kit that would be challenging to build towers with, then place the playing items in a pile. Set the index cards aside until round two. If you're playing this game in a small area, consider using just the cards. Have kids form small groups of three or four and invite each player to choose a playing item from the pile.

LET'S PLAY!

Say: **Raise your hands if you think your team can build the biggest tower in only a few minutes.** Pause for responses, then continue: **When I say "Go!" you'll have three minutes to build the tallest tower you**

PLAYING PIECES

❏ Bible
❏ index cards
❏ crayons
❏ stopwatch or timer
❏ a large variety of Game Kit items

can using the playing pieces in this pile. Begin with the items you have now, then choose one player at a time to retrieve another item and add it to your tower. Keep adding items until time is up or until your tower topples. If the tower topples, sit quietly and watch other teams build. Ready? Go!

If a team topples its tower and others need the building materials, let them use items from the toppled tower. Many, if not most, of the towers will have tumbled by the time you halt the building. Call time after three minutes, then say: **I saw some impressive building crews at work, but I notice that some of the towers have toppled.** Ask:

✔ *Why did these towers tumble?*

✔ *How did you feel if your tower tumbled, especially if you thought your team could build a very tall one?*

Say: The people of Babel had a similar problem. They thought they could build a tall tower to reach God and be like him. But their pride got in the way, and God made their tower tumble. Let's take a moment to remind ourselves what being humble means and why we're to be humble before the Lord.

PEP TALK

Invite volunteers to read aloud Proverbs 8:13; 11:2; 16:5, 18. Then ask:

✔ *What does it mean to be prideful? to be humble?*

✔ *How can being full of pride hurt us? our relationship with God?*

✔ *What can we do to keep from being prideful? to develop humility?*

Say: **It's important to recognize that we're not the biggest, the wisest, or the most powerful—only God is. We want to be sure we're giving God the glory for being the best, not ourselves. Being humble means admitting that we're not the smartest and declaring that God alone is the best. The people of Babel learned the hard way that God is the wisest and most powerful—and we can learn from their mistake.**

Let's build tall towers again, this time using index cards. If your tower tumbles, shout "God is best!" Then choose a card from the pile and write a sentence that gives God glory for being the wisest or the most powerful.

ADD AN ACTION

Exodus 20:2-17; Matthew 22:37-40; Romans 2:13

ENERGY LEVEL: Medium to low
PLAYING TIME: 15 minutes

GOAL OF THE GAME: Repeat the list of actions in their correct order.

Prior to playing, let kids each choose a playing item from the Game Kit, then form a large circle.

LET'S PLAY!

Say: **How good at remembering are you? Well, let's find out with this goofy game called Add an Action. One player will make up an action using her playing item—for example, tossing it in the air and clapping one time. Pay attention, because the next person will use his item to repeat the action before him, then add his own! We'll travel around the circle and see if the first person can repeat everyone's actions in order. If you forget someone's action, call on that player to repeat his move.**

Go around the circle one time, then say: **Wow! That was a lot to remember, wasn't it! We kept adding more and more actions until the list of actions we had to remember was hard to follow. God knows that sometimes we have too many rules to remember and that, if we can't remember them, we can't follow them. That's why God gave us ten simple rules to obey. Let's take a moment to review the ten important rules, or commandments, God gave us to obey.**

PLAYING PIECES

❏ Bible
❏ a playing item from the Game Kit for each child

PEP TALK

Read aloud Exodus 20:2-17 and Romans 2:13. Then ask:
✔ *Why did God give us the Ten Commandments?*
✔ *How can obeying God's rules keep us safe? happy? close to God?*

✔ *Why do you think God didn't give us lots more rules?*

Say: **God gave us the Ten Commandments to help us live safely and happily. God could have given even more rules, but he knew these ten were the most important ones there are. Later on, when Jesus came to love and teach us, he summarized the Ten Commandments into two easy-to-remember rules.** Read Matthew 22:37-40, then say: **Jesus knew that the rules could be summed up and kept if we love God and others more than ourselves, just as he did.**

Let's play Add an Action again, and this time we'll add a praise word for the Lord with each action. You might say "joyful" or "powerful" or "almighty" as you do your action. By the time we travel around our circle, we'll have a whole list of praise and thank-yous to God for giving us such important rules to live by!

COPYCATS

John 13:15, 34; 1 Corinthians 10:31–11:1; 1 Peter 2:21, 22

ENERGY LEVEL: Low
PLAYING TIME: 10 minutes

GOAL OF THE GAME: Follow the leader as she taps out catchy rhythms.

Prior to playing, have each child choose either a plastic plate or tumbler, then hand everyone a plastic spoon. (If you have more than 12 kids, have some kids tap on paper plates or the paint stir sticks.)

LET'S PLAY!

Have kids stand in a circle and repeat the following rhythm several times as you say these words: **One, two, stomp your feet—clap your hands; have you got the beat?** After kids have the stomp-and-clap rhythm down, say: **You followed that rhythm well. Let's play a rhythmic game of Copycats. I'll choose someone to use his spoon to tap out a rhythm on a plastic tumbler or plate, then**

PLAYING PIECES

- ❏ Bible
- ❏ 8 plastic tumblers
- ❏ 4 plastic plates
- ❏ plastic spoons

the rest of us will join in the beat. **When I point to someone else, that player will become the new leader. We'll continue until everyone has led our rollicking rhythm band.**

Continue creating new rhythms to follow until everyone has had a turn to be the leader of the band. Encourage kids to be creative with clapping, tapping, and banging their rhythm instruments. Then say: **What a splendid band we had going there—you followed each leader very well! It was easy to hear if someone wasn't in sync with the rhythm, though. But once everyone was tapping out the same pattern and following the leader, everything sounded great. It's the same way when we're following Jesus. If we're not following our perfect leader in the correct ways, it really shows in our lives. Let's take a brief intermission and learn about the importance of following our heavenly leader.**

PEP TALK

Read aloud John 13:15, 34; 1 Corinthians 10:31–11:1; and 1 Peter 2:21, 22. Then ask:

✔ *Why is it important to follow Jesus in all we say and do?*
✔ *What might happen if we don't follow and obey Jesus?*
✔ *What did Jesus do that we want to follow and imitate?*
✔ *In what ways is following Jesus a way to tell him we love him? have faith in him as our leader?*

Say: **When we follow Jesus, we stay in rhythm with what Jesus wants us to do. Jesus was loving, kind, and accepting of others. We can follow and do the same. Jesus obeyed God and learned his Word. We can follow and do the same. Jesus forgave others and didn't judge them, and so can we. Let's follow this rhythm to remind us to follow the perfect leader in all we do and say!**

Lead kids in tapping out a rhythm to the following rhyme.

One, two, tap your feet—
When we follow Jesus, we've got the beat!

PLAYING TIPS

✔ *If there's time, encourage kids to form small groups to write rhymes about following Jesus with accompanying claps and taps. Perform the rhythm-raps and end with rounds of lively applause.*

108

NUMBER LINEUP

Romans 12:12; Galatians 5:22; 2 Peter 1:5-8

ENERGY LEVEL: Low
PLAYING TIME: 15 minutes

GOAL OF THE GAME: Subtract all the numbers from your opponents.

Prior to playing, use crayons to number the paper plates from 1 to 10. Make the numbers very large and bold on the plates! Have kids form two teams and stand about 6 feet apart. When each team has a turn to hold the plates, you may need to have some players hold two plates, depending on the size of your teams.

PLAYING PIECES

❑ Bible
❑ 10 paper plates
❑ crayons
❑ rolling cube (see page 6)

LET'S PLAY!

Say: **This is a fun number game, the object of which is to subtract as many numbers as possible from your opponents. One team will hold the numbered plates in order from 1 to 10. The other team will toss the rolling cube two times each turn and, depending on the roll, decide which numbers to take away from the opponents. For example, if a 6 and a 4 are rolled, a team could take away the number 10 plate (6+4), the number 2 plate (6-4), or the 6 and 4 plates. You can decide, then roll again. Each team will roll until they cannot subtract any more plates from the number line.**

Play two rounds so each team has a turn to roll the cube and subtract plates. Then say: **That's a fun game that takes some real decision-making thought. You know, all choices should be made in the same way—with lots of thought**

Team 1

Team 2

as we keep clearly in mind what God would want us to do. There are lots of things we can subtract from our lives that would make following God easier. And the best way to see what we should subtract from our lives is to see what God wants us to keep in our lives!

PEP TALK

Read aloud Romans 12:12; Galatians 5:22; and 2 Peter 1:5-8. Then ask:
- ✔ *What things does God want us to have in our lives?*
- ✔ *What negative things can we subtract from our lives?* (Help kids name actions and attitudes such as deceit, bad language, impatience, unkindness, and being judgmental.)
- ✔ *How can working to add positive things to our lives draw us closer to God? stop negatives from creeping back in?*

Say: **It's important to keep and grow good things such as honesty, kindness, patience, perseverance, and faith in our lives. When we work to add the good traits God desires us to have, it makes it harder for the negatives to be in our lives. And when the negatives are subtracted, we discover how close we are to God! Now *that's* math I like!**

Let's play Number Lineup again and name negatives we want to subtract from our lives each time a number plate is removed. Then we'll end by rolling numbers to add back up to ten as we name good things to add to our lives.

HOP-N-STOP

Luke 10:27; Galatians 5:13

ENERGY LEVEL: Medium
PLAYING TIME: 10-15 minutes

GOAL OF THE GAME: Be the first team to hop through the game grid and score the highest number of points.

Prior to playing, use masking tape to create two hopscotch grids (see the illustration on page 111). Make the squares in the grid about a foot square and place the grids about 4 feet apart. Place stir sticks about 3 feet away from the number 1 boxes.

These will be the tossing lines. Have kids form two teams and stand behind the tossing line. Hand each team two crayons and an index card.

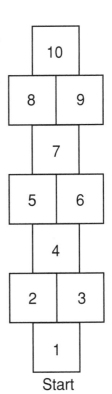

PLAYING PIECES

❑ Bible
❑ masking tape
❑ 4 crayons
❑ 2 index cards
❑ 2 paint stir sticks

LET'S PLAY!

Say: **How many of you have ever played Hopscotch? This relay race is very similar. In Hop-n-Stop, we'll take turns tossing crayons onto the game grids. Write the number you toss on the index card, then hop on one foot on the single boxes and two feet on the double boxes. When you reach the crayon, stop and pick it up without losing your balance. If you stumble or lose your balance, you must scratch out your number and toss again. We'll play until every team has hopped, then we'll add up the scores.**

After adding up the scores, give a lively round of applause for the team with the most points. Then say: **Hop-n-Stop is a fun relay race, and it reminds me of the Bible story called the Good Samaritan. Who can retell that story?** Allow time for kids to read or retell the parable of the Good Samaritan from Luke 10:30-35. Then say: **The Good Samaritan stopped to help the hurt man before going on. Let's take a moment to see why Jesus wants us to be hop-n-stop helpers.**

PEP TALK

Invite a volunteer to read aloud Luke 10:27 and Galatians 5:13b. Then ask:

✔ *In what ways did Jesus help others?*
✔ *How can we help others as Jesus did?*
✔ *Why is it important to be willing to help someone instead of just ignoring their needs?*

Say: **The Good Samaritan stopped to help someone in need before hopping on his way, just as Jesus always did. Stopping to help shows caring and loving-kindness—just as Jesus had for us. During** the next week, look for times you can hop-n-stop to help someone in need. Maybe it's through a smile, helping with a chore, or saying an encouraging word. But each time we stop to help someone, we're doing just what Jesus would do!

Play Hop-n-Stop again, then end with high fives for everyone!